DISABILITY AND EMPIRE:

CLASS, US IMPERIALISM, AND THE STRUGGLE FOR DISABILITY JUSTICE

JOYCE CHEDIAC, JANE CUTTER,
JOHN PETER DALY, AND SUNIL FREEMAN

Published in September 2024 by
1804 Books, New York, NY

1804Books.com

ISBN: 979-8-9882602-8-8
Library of Congress Control Number: 2024939613

Cover by Josh Mayfield

TABLE OF CONTENTS

Dedication	v
Introduction	vii
The Social Construction of 'Disability' in the US	1
Every Advance Requires a Fight	11
Building Solidarity Between Care Workers and Clients	27
Killer and Disabler of Millions	37
The Status of Rights for People with Disabilities	47
A Glimpse into a Liberating Future	55
A Socialist United States and the Liberation of People with Disabilities	65
Endnotes	71

DEDICATION

We dedicate this booklet to the memory of our coauthor John Peter Daly who died June 28, 2023, age fifty-eight. A lifelong organizer, he committed himself to building the Party for Socialism and Liberation (PSL) in many parts of the United States. At the time of his death, he had been living in Baton Rouge, Louisiana, since 2016 where he was a much-loved member of the PSL's Gulf Coast Branch.

In his later years, John suffered from a traumatic brain injury and had subsequent surgeries that left him an incomplete quadriplegic. His disability compromised his mobility, left him experiencing frequent and debilitating pain, and made him a victim of the inhumane capitalist health-care system.

Many others would have given up organizing under these circumstances. Not John. He saw what others might deem his "personal" challenges as products of the capitalist system, and sought to use these challenges to connect with other workers and advance the struggle.

In 2020, a few years after his injury, living in Baton Rouge, he organized other people with disabilities, and as he describes in the third chapter of this book, John envisioned a model for organizing the low-wage workers who are employed as caregivers for people with disabilities.

John Peter Daly understood that struggle changes consciousness, and that the people have the ability to unite and overcome any challenges if under the right conditions and with the right consciousness. He fought every day of his life. We are honored to carry forth his legacy.

INTRODUCTION

This booklet is an effort by the Party for Socialism and Liberation to bring visibility to the struggle for the liberation of people with disabilities, adding an internationalist class perspective and making people with disabilities the subject, not the object, of history.

A lot has been written about this topic, from highly theoretical and academic works to personal accounts of individuals with disabilities and everything in between. In reviewing the history of the struggle for the rights of disabled people in the United States, we write about how this movement, like so many other important social movements, took inspiration from the Black liberation struggle of the 1950s, '60s, and '70s. The progenitors of today's disability rights movement saw their struggle as interconnected to other struggles, because most disabled people are part of the working class and/or members of other oppressed groups and communities. In fact, it has been said that disability is the only category of special oppression that anyone can become a member of, at any time in their life.

In chapter 1, "Rationalizing Oppression: The Social Construction of 'Disability' in the US," we discuss the social construction of disability and the ways in which the concept of disability has been used to justify colonialism, racism, and sexism. We explain how, contrary to an everyday understanding, having an impairment (for lack of a better word) of physical or cognitive functions is not itself a disability. Disability is what happens when an impairment collides with a society that has barriers to full and equal participation. These barriers are both literal, in the case of inaccessible architecture and public spaces, or socio-cultural, in the case of discrimination, lack of accommodation, support, and so on.

In chapter 2, we outline the origins of the militant movement for the rights and liberation of people with disabilities. Highlighted is the inspiration this movement took from the movement for Black liberation and the LGBTQ, women's, and anti-war struggles of the time, defining disability issues as those of "civil rights" and "liberation."

Chapter 3 delves into coauthor John Daly's story as a seasoned socialist organizer faced with becoming disabled at mid-life. Central to his experiences has been an ongoing struggle to receive appropriate home-based support, along with the understanding that these care workers are super-exploited, and so we briefly outline past and present efforts to organize home care workers. We also introduce strategies used in the farmworkers' movement that might address some of the specific challenges in this organizing space, while also focusing on ways to resolve the seeming contradiction between people with disabilities and the home care workers they rely on.

Chapter 4 highlights the bloody role of US imperialism in causing countless physical and mental health impairments leading to disabilities around the world: among the people of the nations invaded, occupied, and oppressed by the US, as well as the US military personnel, the cannon fodder of imperialism, who carry out these criminal wars. We analyze the environmental devastation caused by imperialist war and subsequent health impairments leading to disability as a result of toxic substances such as Agent Orange and depleted uranium.

In chapter 5, we return to the US to look at the state of disability rights today, decades after the passage of the Americans with Disabilities Act (ADA). Enforcement of the ADA is an ongoing struggle, carried out piecemeal. We uplift the contributions of two great women leaders in the struggle for liberation, each of whom died as a direct result of the capitalist system's prioritization of profit over human need.

In chapter 6, we examine the gains for people with disabilities in socialist countries, and in chapter 7, we develop our vision for a socialist future in which people with disabilities are liberated from the socially imposed constraints that limit them from full participation in society.

We hope to stimulate a discussion about what the future could be for people with disabilities under socialism. Instead of poverty, discrimination, exclusion, and often-ignored medical needs, we could have quality, comprehensive, and universal health care. We could have beautiful public and private spaces made accessible with universal design. We could create opportunities for all to contribute in their own way to meaningful and connected communities. We believe that people with physical, cognitive, or mental health impairments have much to offer society. Whether this takes the form of meaningful full- or part-time paid employment, community leadership and advocacy, cultural expressions of poetry, art, music, and so on, every person is intrinsically valuable and can influence society in a positive way.

This view goes counter to the ethos of capitalism, in which the value of a person is measured monetarily. In a system based on competition, not cooperation, individualism is a primary value. People "of value" who are seen as being successful are believed to have "made it on their own." Of course, we know that this is not really true: most "overnight successes" especially in the world of capitalist business, come from family wealth and privilege (think of Bill Gates and Elon Musk). Even people who are relatively successful in our society, who have gone to college and work in the profession they studied, may forget that they did not "make it" all on their own; countless others contributed to their growth and development.

We all stand on the shoulders of giants, those that preceded us, who made our gains possible. Each "successful" person needed different kinds of help at different points within their development. So, it must be for all people in a socialist society. Different people need different kinds of support in order to achieve their potential and live fulfilled lives. Instead of uplifting some individuals over the many, a socialist United States would have the resources to provide appropriate education and other forms of support to meet the unique needs of each community member. In this way, we could all benefit from what today is the untapped potential of countless members of the working class, both those with and without disabilities.

In a society based on sustainable planning to meet people's needs, neighborhood solidarity could be the norm. We have a vision of a society in which helping others is a respected career, in which we can all learn from and help each other to grow and develop to our potential. The present may seem bleak, but we have optimism for a future where, with unity and solidarity, we can achieve liberation for all.

THE SOCIAL CONSTRUCTION OF 'DISABILITY' IN THE US

The Centers for Disease Control and Prevention (CDC) estimates that sixty-one million adults in the US live with some kind of disability.[1] This number excludes the many family members and others who may not have disabilities but "live with a disability" because they struggle to support their family members with little or no government support.

The National Institute of Mental Health (NIMH) estimated in 2020 that 52.9 million adults, nearly one in five of the population, live with a mental illness in the US.[2] In 2020, an estimated 5.6 percent of the adults in the US, 14.2 million people, had a severe mental illness. Given this society's extreme inequality, it should be no surprise that some groups suffer more than others. Poverty, racism, and lack of health care add to the challenges many people with disabilities face. One in three adults with disabilities between eighteen to forty-four years old has a health-care need that was unmet due to cost in the past year. A similar number have no regular health-care provider. One in four adults with a disability between forty-five to sixty-four years old did not have a routine medical checkup in 2021.[3]

Historical Perspectives

People have faced serious physical, cognitive, and/or mental challenges for as long as humans have existed. Societies have struggled to understand why some people have impairments and what their relationship to the broader community should be. These impairments have often been compounded, to deadly effect, by societal attitudes, laws, and state-sanctioned violence. In fact, "disability" is a social construct and has had different meanings at different times and in different places. For example, we are led to believe that early human societies were always brutal and warlike with each other, did not value people with disabilities, and even threw them away. Popular belief is that compassion and care for people with disabilities and others is a product of what they call "civilization."

Archeological evidence strongly suggests otherwise: that early humans supported people with disabilities who probably would not have otherwise survived. Skeletal remains dating from the Old Stone Age show people with severe disabilities such as spina bifida, congenital hip dislocation, and osteomyelitis living into adulthood.

In 2007, archaeologists found the bones of a young man who lived four thousand years ago in northern Vietnam. He had fused vertebrae, weak bones, and other evidence that he was paralyzed from the waist down before adolescence due to a degenerative disease. He had little if any use of his arms and could not have fed himself or kept himself clean—yet this disabled person lived another ten years.[4] The scientists who found the young man's remains concluded that the people in this Neolithic society took the time and care to tend to his every need. The *New York Times* says, "Not only does his care indicate tolerance and cooperation in his culture, but suggests that he himself had a sense of his worth and a strong will to live," which would have been needed to survive with such severe ailments.

About thirty similar remains have been found in areas ranging from Europe to Asia, the US, and the Middle East. Some remains go back forty-five thousand years and show disease and pathology so severe that the affected people must have needed and gotten round-the-clock care.[5] These archeological findings of what appears to be tender care for the sick and the aged suggest the exact opposite of the general beliefs about the callousness of early human societies.

'Disability' as Social Alienation

While these ancient ancestors cannot tell us what their values were, there are other ways we can learn about the care given to people with disabilities across culture and time. In the book *Disability History of the United States,* author Kim E. Nielsen gives voice to the Indigenous people of this continent and their views on disability. In traditional cultures, Nielsen explains, everyone was believed to have a gift, skill, ability, or purpose. When individuals, communities, and the world are in harmony, individuals share their gifts and benefit from the gifts of others.

Most pre-Columbian Indigenous communities had no word or concept for what we call disability. For example, if someone described today as being "cognitively impaired" was a good water carrier, that was the person's gift and was appreciated. There was no stigma attached, and they were loved and welcomed, according to Nielsen. People were not defined by their ability or disability but by their contribution to the whole. People were appreciated for what they did and the wholeness of their personalities.

Nielsen says that in some tribes, the closest thing to the word "disability" was a relational term. It applied when someone had weak community relations or lacked them, or when a person was removed from or unable to participate in community reciprocity. Today we might call this "alienation." So, if you were alienated from society, that was a disability. This sophisticated and compassionate concept developed in a society where most people lived as equals. Their survival as a group depended on working together and sharing food and resources.

While class society has certainly brought technological development, it has not brought compassion. It has brought inequality, stratification, judgment, and great suffering to most people. For example, Christopher Columbus came from a feudal society that treated peasants as little more than rural slaves.[6] He gave his view of the people he met in the Americas in his journal, writing: "They should be good servants. . . . with fifty men they can all be subjugated and made to do what is required of them . . . "[7] This representative of "civilization" went on to enslave Native people and steal their land.

A survey of the views of Indigenous people with impairments today in Australia, New Zealand, and Mexico, published in 2018 in *Disability Studies Quarterly*,[8] found their perspective on disability to be very similar to those reported by Nielsen. They believed each person is unique and valued for their contributions to the whole rather than being defined by any impairments. Indigenous people with impairments who were polled "celebrated individual uniqueness perceiving that individuals' bodies, minds, and spirits are part of a continuum. . . . " They "separate their social identity from their experience of living with impairments, and their narratives revealed that they interpreted disability as a Western construct and a current manifestation of ongoing colonization." This is because the "Western construct," the construct of capitalism/imperialism, stigmatizes people with disabilities.

Marx and Disability

Although Karl Marx and Frederick Engels did not specifically address the treatment of disability in society, they recognized the damage capitalist production inflicted on workers. In volume 3 of *Capital*, Marx wrote that capitalism "squanders human lives . . . and not only blood and flesh, but also nerve and brain."

Designed to maximize profits for a tiny class of owners, capitalism offers a bleak set of options to the entire working class. This is even more profoundly true for people with disabilities. Accommodations that would enable them to work are seen as overhead expenses by the capitalists, a burden to be avoided. Because under capitalism, workers are only valued for their ability to generate surplus value, and people with disabilities are seen as having no intrinsic value. This particular social construct of disability developed with the growth of capitalism.

Disability as the Inability to Perform Labor

In the US colonial and early national eras of the seventeenth and eighteenth centuries, when the economy was mostly based on farming, the primary definition of disability was the inability to perform labor. With illness and farming-related and other kinds of accidents widespread, people who were missing limbs, hard of hearing, blind, or with mobility limits were fairly common. But most could be worked into existing labor patterns of home-based cottage industries, and most were cared for by their families.[9] Depending on the impairment, they could plant fields, hunt, spin, weave, sail, mind children, build a barrel, etc.

People of this time saw "disability" as applying primarily to mental illness severe enough to make it impossible for a person to work or work consistently, or which made them disruptive to society. If a family could not care for such a person, the municipality often took it on. There was no shame associated with disability.

The seventeenth and eighteenth centuries were not gentler than later periods. Conditions were harsh, and the social order was enforced through violence. But the material conditions of smaller-scale rural communities, where everyone's labor was needed to maintain a household or a farm, lent itself to a more communal outlook. Labor flexibility was needed in order to ensure that all the work got done.

As capitalism/imperialism developed with its sharp class divisions and exploitation of the many for the benefit of the few, it reshaped the concept of disability in a way that justified this inequality. People with disabilities were not defined by their personalities or contributions, but by that disability. They were seen as flawed, in need of fixing, and inferior to those who do not have impairments. Ableism, with its harmful stereotypes, generalizations, and misconceptions concerning people with disabilities, became a tool to justify oppression, just like racism and sexism. Ableism was used to justify not only the oppression of people with impairments, but of whole other groups as well.

Disability Used to Rationalize Slavery, Sexism, and Capitalist Exploitation

After the US Civil War, the completion of the intercontinental railroad and rapid industrialization brought unprecedented wealth to a few from the exploitation of the many. People with physical disabilities who had earlier worked gainfully at home could not travel to or work in the new factories, which now defined the economy.

At the same time, dangerous working conditions in the plants and mines and on the railroads and docks disabled workers by the thousands. Most were then summarily fired without compensation with the bosses often attributing disability to worker carelessness rather than to the speedups and hazards to which they were subjected. Bosses blame workers in the same way to this day. It took the trade unions to fight for safe working conditions on the job and economic compensation and pensions for those injured.

As class contradictions sharpened, "disability" took on a political meaning. The philosophy of social Darwinism attributed the enormous economic disparities between rich and poor to the deficiencies of the poor.[10] Gender, race, and class criteria were used to justify social and political exploitation and by defining vast sectors of the population as disabled.

Fueled by economics, racism, sexism, class oppression, and ableism, among other forms of bigotry, capitalists marked slaves, Indigenous people, immigrants, and women as unfit, justifying their oppression, and also denying them the right to vote.[11] Disability was used to justify the enslavement of Africans, whom the ruling class labeled as inferior and best suited for enslavement.[12]

Disability Constructed as Unsightly, Disgusting, and Criminal

One of the most infamous examples of discrimination were the laws aimed at "unsightly beggars," i.e., down-and-out working-class people and people with disabilities. In 1867, San Francisco passed the first of what became known as "ugly laws." Other cities, including Chicago, Reno, and Omaha had similar laws. Text of the San Francisco law included:

> Any person who is diseased, maimed, mutilated, or in any way deformed so as to be an unsightly or disgusting object or an improper person to be allowed in or on the streets, highways, thoroughfares, or public places in the City or County of San Francisco shall not therein or thereon expose himself or herself to public view.[13]

"Improper and not allowed in and on the streets" was also interpreted as referring to a person's race, gender, national origins, lack of funds, or sexual orientation.

Likewise, until the passage of the Education for All Handicapped Children Act in 1975 (now known as the Individuals with Disabilities Education Act or IDEA), school children with disabilities were routinely excluded from public schools.

'Disability' Justifies Colonial Conquests

Colonial conquests were justified by extreme ableism and racism, defining oppressed people as mentally disabled.[14] For example, Rudyard Kipling's now infamous poem "The White Man's Burden: The United States and the Philippine Islands" urged the 1899 US colonial invasion of the Philippines, resulting in widespread violence, famine, and disease that killed as many as one million Filipinos in the three-year war of US conquest and annexation.[15] Often called his hymn to imperialism, the poem justifies imperialist conquest by slandering those eventually subjected to imperialism's rule as "half devil half child" and weaponizing disability in the service of colonial interests.[16]

Eugenics and Forced Sterilization

In the twentieth century, people with disabilities were among the more than sixty thousand who were forcibly sterilized in thirty-two states across the US.[17] Backers of the racist and fake "science" of eugenics proposed to protect society by not allowing people with "inferior" genes to procreate.

Because eugenicists deemed Anglo-Saxon and Nordic genes to be superior, Black and Indigenous people, many immigrants, and people with disabilities were among the groups targeted. In 1907, Indiana passed the world's first sterilization law, followed by thirty-one other states.[18]

Hitler closely studied the United States, particularly eugenics and Jim Crow legal segregation, as he rose to power in Germany. People with disabilities were among the millions slaughtered in the Nazi death camps, a brutal and logical result of the eugenic concept applied to Europeans.

The Criminalization of Mental Illness

People with mental illness have been shunned or persecuted. In 1752, Quakers in Philadelphia opened an early hospital with a basement area for treating mental illness. Additional hospitals were built in the following decades, including in Williamsburg, Virginia (1792) and New York City (1793). The Eastern Lunatic Asylum, opened in 1824 in Lexington, Kentucky, was the first such hospital west of the Appalachian Mountains. Now named Eastern State Hospital, it is still in operation. Although such institutions may have been created with good intentions, many did little more than locking severely disturbed people away from society. Once institutionalized, there was no legal right to treatment. The institutions also became catchalls for the poor, orphans, alcoholics, pregnant women without husbands, people with epilepsy or with developmental disabilities or on the autism spectrum, and others.[19]

In the mid-nineteenth century, Dorothea Dix advocated for better treatment of people with mental illnesses. Dix helped to establish or expand thirty institutions for the treatment of mental illness.[20] A long campaign for the right to treatment and a series of reports exposing harsh conditions in the mid-twentieth century led to a movement to release patients into supportive community housing where they could receive therapy and at least partially reintegrate into society. In theory, this was an admirable development. Unfortunately, inadequate funding for planned community support meant many people ended up living on the street or, ultimately, in prison.[21]

Today nearly half of the people in the vast US prison and jail system have a mental illness.[22] The institution that houses the greatest number of people diagnosed with a mental health disability is the US jail and prison system, with Chicago's Cook County Jail, the Los Angeles County Jail, and New York City's Rikers Island being the largest mental health facilities in the US.[23] Additionally, half of the people killed by the police have a disability.[24]

Disability Rights, an Outgrowth of the Civil Rights Movement

It takes an organized, militant effort to push back against such deeply entrenched, state-sanctioned bigotry and win basic rights for people with disabilities. As the civil rights movement against racist laws gained momentum in the 1950s, 1960s, and 1970s, related struggles intensified to demand basic rights for women, the LGBTQ community, and people with disabilities.

Disabled activists fought for their human and civil rights. They saw "disability" as something imposed on top of any impairments they might have. They defined "disability" as "a social condition of discrimination, an unmerited stigma, which needlessly harms and restricts the lives of those with disabilities and results in economic disparities, social isolation, and oppression."[25]

Passage of the Americans with Disabilities Act (ADA) in 1990 was a step forward in that ongoing struggle. The 2020 documentary film *Crip Camp* describes that struggle, which included the 1977 takeover of a federal building in San Francisco to demand that the government enforce Section 504, a law protecting people with disabilities. As powerfully shown in the documentary, members of the Black Panther Party delivered hot meals to the demonstrators, and members of the International Brotherhood of Teamsters showed their solidarity by transporting wheelchair users to similar protests in New York City.

While far from perfect, the ADA has helped to increase access to jobs, education, transportation, and participation in society for people with disabilities. The struggle continues for the enforcement of existing laws and fighting for full rights. As a result of those struggles, people with disabilities play a more prominent role in society and are joining in other movements for liberation and equality.

Laws like the Americans with Disabilities Act were hard won through struggle, but once won, a new struggle began to get them enforced under capitalism or to get the funds to implement them adequately. For example, some workers with disabilities can find fulfilling employment, but many do not. Many are super-exploited through a provision of US labor law. Even though it violates the ADA, employers can apply to the Department of Labor for certificates that allow them to pay a subminimum wage to people with disabilities. According to the US Commission on Civil Rights, one hundred thousand people working under such conditions received an average hourly wage of $3.34 between 2017 and 2018. This is less than half the already inadequate $7.25 per hour federal minimum wage.[26]

Fighting for Socialism

While the struggle for reforms is crucial, the capitalist system is simply not designed to accept people with disabilities as full members of society. To guarantee full rights, many people with disabilities are joining with others in the fight to establish a socialist system where human rights, not profits, are primary.

In *Capitalism and Disability,* Marxist disability rights advocate Marta Russell points out that under capitalism, there is no broad right to be free of hunger or to have shelter. Socialism regards these as basic human rights for all people, along with the right to a job at a living wage and health care.

Sicko, Michael Moore's 2007 documentary film about the US health-care system, includes a powerful section comparing US and Cuban health care. It follows several first responders who were severely disabled while conducting rescue work in the aftermath of September 11, 2001. The US government abandoned them as they struggled to get the health care they needed and to make ends meet. Moore arranged for them to go to Cuba, a socialist country, where they received extensive treatment and medicine at almost no cost, just as would have been given to anyone in Cuba. The distinction between the two systems could not have been illustrated more clearly.

EVERY ADVANCE REQUIRES A FIGHT

The passage of the Americans with Disability Act (ADA) in 1990 was a landmark achievement, so it is understandably the focus of considerable attention even today. It's important to recognize that there were decades of struggle that preceded the ADA, not to mention the ongoing fight after its passage to get it implemented.

The National Association of the Deaf, founded in 1880, was the first national organization advocating for disabled people in the US. From its beginnings, it was run by deaf people and advocated for deaf rights.[27] It is active today, advocating for deaf and hard-of-hearing people on various issues, including education, employment, health care, technology, telecommunications, youth leadership, and more. It also works in coalition with national cross-disability organizations.

Many schoolchildren in the US first learn of disability through stories about Helen Keller, an advocate for justice who was deaf and blind. Although she became something of a celebrity, the popularized image of her taught in schools did not include the fact that she was a socialist and opposed US involvement in World War I.[28]

In 1924, Keller wrote in a letter:

> As long as I confine my activities to social service and the blind, they compliment me extravagantly, calling me "archpriestess of the sightless," "wonder woman," and a "modern miracle." But when it comes to a discussion of poverty, and I maintain that it is the result of wrong economics—that the industrial system under which we live is

11

at the root of much of the physical deafness and blindness
in the world—that is a different matter![29]

Keller was involved in many struggles, including women's suffrage,
abortion rights, labor unions, disability rights, civil rights, and fighting against the imperialist war machine. She was a founder of the
American Civil Liberties Union.

The American Federation of the Physically Handicapped (AFPH),
founded in 1940, worked to end job discrimination, advocated for the
passage of legislation, and called for the establishment of an annual
Employ the Physically Handicapped Week. It was significant as the
first national political organization that combined different physical
disabilities.[30] Also significantly, it excluded mental health conditions.

Most AFPH members were themselves disabled and advocated for
active inclusion in society. In their literature, they described themselves as a group that "refrained from using the 'sob-story' appeal
since it represented those who, despite a physical disability, wanted to
earn their way."[31]

Fighting Infantilizing Stereotypes

People with disabilities have long struggled against perceptions that
they are unfortunate victims, are less than fully human, and are only
deserving of pity and charity, narratives that corporate media has
amplified. This demeaning and infantilizing view is perhaps best
illustrated by the comedian Jerry Lewis and his long-running Labor
Day telethons, which ran for more than twenty hours on television
and raised nearly $2.5 billion for the Muscular Dystrophy Association
(MDA) over the years.

These were gaudy shows. Hosted by Lewis from 1966 to 2010,
they featured appearances by major celebrities, musical stars, jokes,
and especially by "Jerry's Kids," children with muscular dystrophy
who were paraded on stage to get people to pledge money. Lewis
responded angrily when activists spoke out about the harm caused by
such demeaning depictions. Mike Ervin, an activist featured on the
show as a child, noted:

Lewis and the Muscular Dystrophy Association wallowed
in the pity approach. The basic message they hammered

into the heads of American viewers year after year was that disabled people are powerless, passive, fragile, child-like, and unable to contribute anything meaningful to society unless we are "cured."[32]

To illustrate just how offensive the depiction was, in 1973, Lewis appealed for donations by picking up a child and announcing: "God goofed, and it's up to us to correct His mistakes."[33]

MDA telethons continued with reduced hours until 2014, with other hosts following Lewis' departure. Despite protests, the telethon began again in 2020 with Kevin Hart hosting.[34] Emily Wolinsky, who had been an MDA Poster Child in the 1980s, wrote a letter to Hart, titled, "Dear Kevin Hart, The MDA is Heartless," condemning the deeply racist structural problems with MDA and other such charita-ble programs.[35] Wolinsky, who is white, wrote:

> The MDA largely ignores Black, brown, and poor kids (and adults) for the same reasons that emphasize why we'll never see any telethons for all the children in Flint, Mich-igan, who became disabled from the poisonous drinking water. Underrepresentation on many, many fronts plagues disability-driven charities due to deeply rooted and racist biases surrounding American Generosity.

While the media and government officials may celebrate the accom-plishments of individuals with disabilities or acts of charity toward them, they do not address systemic oppression. Time and again, there is "not enough money" to ensure access or even meet the most basic needs. When people with disabilities push back against such damag-ing depictions and demand full access to participate in society, they can face fierce opposition.

Movements of the 1960s Provided Inspiration

The fight for Black liberation and full civil rights intensified with the Montgomery bus boycott and other actions in the 1950s. Mil-lions took to the streets in the 1960s opposing the US war in Vietnam. Abroad, people were fighting colonialism in Vietnam, Algeria, and elsewhere.

The liberation struggles associated with the 1960s had a ripple effect that transformed society in the US. These struggles inspired other oppressed groups to organize militant actions: the American Indian Movement, women's, LGBTQ, Chicanos, Puerto Ricans, and other liberation movements. It was only natural that disabled people would also organize and engage in militant struggle.

Camp Jened

In 1952, parents of children with cerebral palsy organized to establish Camp Jened, a summer camp in New York's Catskill mountains. At the time, children with severe disabilities were often warehoused in institutions that controlled their lives and rendered them invisible to mainstream society. Even those not sent to institutions had few opportunities to meet other children.

By the 1970s, the camp, reflecting the times, had moved away from the traditional format to a much more experimental one. By 1971, some called it the "hippie camp," while others said it was sometimes hard to tell the difference between campers and counselors. At Camp Jened, young people with disabilities had a chance to connect with others. Campers had a chance just to be teens, free themselves from stereotypes, and realize their collective strength. It was a liberating experience that had a tremendous impact on the disability rights movement, as Jened alumni were to form the backbone of key struggles to come.

The story of Camp Jened, centered around the activists who attended it and the struggles that followed, is told in the 2020 documentary film *Crip Camp: A Disability Revolution*.[36] The film won the Sundance audience award that year and was nominated for an Academy Award for best documentary feature. The film's creators and supporting organization have created an extensive outreach program, including an educational curriculum, to "extend the knowledge and understanding of disability and of disabled people offered in the film."[37]

Fighting to get Disability Laws Enforced

The passage of the Rehabilitation Act of 1973 was a significant step in the long struggle for disability rights. Then-president Richard Nixon had vetoed the legislation in 1971 and again in 1972, using the all too familiar excuse that it was too costly. He finally signed the legislation when the House and Senate passed a revised version. Section 504 of the act forbids discrimination by employers and lists crucial rights for disabled people, including access to all benefits and services in programs that receive federal funding.

In a related legislative victory, in 1975, Congress passed the Education for All Handicapped Children Act, known now as the Individuals with Disabilities Education Act or IDEA, asserting the right of disabled children to a free, appropriate public education in the least restrictive environment.

The Rehabilitation Act of 1973 was a milestone achievement, won through a long struggle. But it was meaningless unless the federal government activated Section 504 and issued regulations to actually enforce the provisions. Although Nixon signed the Act in 1973, nearly four years passed, and the incoming Carter administration still had not issued those regulations. Even a lawsuit had not forced the government to uphold the terms of the Act. Militant action was called for.

The Twenty-Five-Day Occupation

In 1977, disability activists took to the streets and protested in cities around the country, targeting regional offices of the federal Department of Health Education and Welfare to demand enforceable regulations. These were known as the 504 Protests, after the part of the bill that contained the guidelines needed to be implemented.

In San Francisco, roughly 120 people occupied a federal building for twenty-five days, attracting widespread media attention. Protesters outside supported those on the inside.

The government responded by shutting off the water in an effort to shut down the protest. They also cut off the phone lines in an effort to silence the protesters inside. This was before cell phones existed. The protesters' creative response? Deaf participants used sign language from a window to ensure their message got out. The takeover was the longest takeover and occupation of a federal government building in US history.

The protest might not have been successful without solidarity. Union members, civil rights organizations, some local government officials, churches, members of the gay community, and others sup-

Occupiers and their supporters in San Francisco's Civic Center Plaza celebrate the signing of the Section 504 regulations. Photo: University of California

ported the action by contributing mattresses, blankets, medicines, and other necessities.

The Black Panthers Bring Food

Especially crucial was the help of the Black Panther Party. Brad Lomax, a member of the Oakland Panther branch who had multiple sclerosis since his teens and used a wheelchair, had joined the occupation. He suggested asking for the help of the Panthers. The Panthers responded, bringing the protesters free hot dinners every day and food for the next day's breakfast and lunch. An April 8, 1977, Black Panther Party press release proclaimed the Party's support:

> Along with all fair and good-thinking people, the Black Panther Party gives its full support to Section 504 of the 1973 Rehabilitation Act and calls for President Carter and HEW Secretary Califano to sign guidelines for its implementation as negotiated and agreed to on January 21 of this year. The issue here is human rights—rights of meaningful employment, of education, of basic human survival—of an oppressed minority, the disabled, and handicapped.[38]

The Black Panther newspaper celebrated the victory of the Section 504 protesters. Courtesy of It's About Time Archive.

Lomax founded the Washington, DC, branch of the Black Panther Party and later moved to Oakland. In 1975, he worked with Ed Roberts, a disability activist and founder of the Center for Independent Living (CIL) in Berkeley. Together they created another CIL run by the Black Panthers in East Oakland.[39]

When twenty protestors went to Washington, DC, to directly target government officials and offices, they found no accessible transportation there. The International Association of Machinists offered their support. The union rented a large U-Haul truck and transported the activists wherever needed.

While this shows the importance of solidarity, it also speaks to the urgent need for accessible transportation. If the wheelchair-riding activists wanted to get around in the nation's capital their only option was to sit in the dark in the back of a truck used to haul furniture.[40] The struggle forced Health, Education, and Welfare Department Secretary Joseph Califano to sign the 504 regulations of the ADA on April 28, 1977.

Militant Direct Actions

Many disability rights organizers recognized the value of the militant direct actions that had proved successful in the struggle for Black liberation.

One such group that has forced considerable change and opened access for people with disabilities is ADAPT, which originally stood for Americans Disabled for Accessible Public Transit, and later became Americans Disabled for Attendant Programs Today.[41] One of its founders, Reverend Wade Blank, had been the recreational director for a nursing home in Denver, Colorado. Blank, who was not disabled, assisted a group of disabled residents in moving out of the nursing home and forming their own community. The issue they had to confront: How would they get around? The inaccessibility of public transportation, an enormous obstacle, became a natural target for demonstrations.

Fighting for Wheelchair Access

On July 5 and 6, 1978, they held the country's first public demonstration for wheelchair access on public buses. Nineteen group members blocked public buses, remaining through the night in the first of many such protests.

In 1983, Wade and members of the original group formed ADAPT. They engaged in civil disobedience actions in several cities. In 1987, members of the group began a campaign to force San Francisco buses to become wheelchair accessible. They were opposed by the American Public Transportation Association (APTA), representing the bus industry, which had the mayor's ear.

ADAPT members in wheelchairs surrounded San Francisco City Hall. APTA officials and others had to climb over protesters' wheelchairs to enter the building. When they later tried to use a back exit to leave the building, they discovered that ADAPT members had pushed large trash cans to block passage.[42] Eventually, the ADAPT struggle was successful, and public buses nationwide are now equipped with lifts to permit wheelchair access. It was a tremendous achievement, one people take for granted today that would not have occurred without this militant struggle. Today ADAPT is active in ongoing struggles for disabled people, including the ability to live in accessible and affordable housing in the community rather than being confined to institutions.[43]

Disabled People's Liberation Front

The San Francisco protests that had forced a change, despite stubborn resistance from the APTA and the political establishment, gained

ADAPT protesters block buses at San Francisco's Transbay Terminal, demanding access. Photo: Robert Clay

widespread support. One important group, the Disabled People's Liberation Front (DPLF), expressed solidarity from Boston by having eight members in wheelchairs join the San Francisco protesters. The DPLF, formed in the late 1970s, and led by James Brooks, was well known for its protests in Boston. Through militant struggle, they prevailed in forcing Boston movie theaters to become wheelchair accessible. DPLF members used highly visible actions to gain support. They chained their wheelchairs together to block traffic in front of the State House to protest steep price increases for a transport system serving people with disabilities. DPLF also consistently expressed solidarity with other struggles, joining picket lines of striking workers and anti-war and gay rights protests.

1988 Gallaudet Protest

The Deaf President Now protests of 1988 at Gallaudet University in Washington, DC, signaled a rising militancy in the deaf community. The university was founded in 1864 as the only university for deaf and hard-of-hearing students worldwide. In 1988, the university's Board of Trustees was considering three candidates for university president. Two of the final candidates were deaf. Many students, alumni, and supporters had strongly urged the university to break with the past and select the first deaf president of the university. Many capable deaf people had the necessary administrative skills and experience. As a university specifically for deaf people, the idea had strong support.

Students were outraged when on March 6, 1988, the trustees announced that they had selected the one hearing candidate, Elisabeth Zinser. They learned about the selection through a press release distributed by the University's Public Relations Office. Hundreds of students on campus blocked Florida Avenue, a major thoroughfare. Then they marched to the Mayflower Hotel where the Board of Trustees was meeting, disrupting the proceedings and demanding a meeting. Board Chair Jane Spilman agreed to meet with them on campus the following day. The students then marched to the White House, and then the Capitol building before returning to campus. The following day, students drove cars to the campus entrances and deflated the tires.

Supported by many alumni, staff, and faculty, they went on strike. They presented the trustees with four demands: (1) Elisabeth Zinser must resign and a deaf person be selected president; (2) Jane Spilman must step down as chairperson of the Board of Trustees; (3) deaf people must constitute a 51 percent majority on the Board; and (4) there would no reprisals against any student or employee involved in the protest.

The intense week of protest included rallies, meetings with officials and supporters, and blockades of the campus. It quickly drew local and then national news coverage. Students proclaimed victory and ended their protest after one week when the trustees agreed to all four demands. Dr. I. King Jordan was named Gallaudet University's first deaf president.[44]

Direct Action for the ADA

Organizers who push for societal improvements through legislative action are well aware of many obstacles. Politicians serve the interests of the wealthy and powerful donors who fund their campaigns. They can speak in support of widely popular legislation while working to undermine chances for actual passage. We still don't have universal health care, a liveable minimum wage, or affordable housing, despite all the politicians' claims that they serve the people.

Many people and organizations struggled to enact the passage of the Americans with Disabilities Act, landmark legislation that would help counteract the widespread oppression of people with disabilities. In the winter of 1990, it became obvious that the legislation had become stalled in the House of Representatives Committee on Public Works and Transportation.

The Capitol Crawl

Realizing that the act was threatened, hundreds of activists converged on Washington, DC, protesting at the White House and the Capitol building. On March 12, 1990, several dozen activists abandoned their canes, crutches, and other mobility aids and slowly crawled up the steps of the US Capitol building. What became known as the Capitol Crawl protest starkly illustrated the obstacles to access they constantly faced. It shamed the politicians who were blocking the passage of the act.

Ultimately the protests were successful, and President George H. W. Bush signed the ADA into law on July 26, 1990. The ADA is a civil rights law that prohibits discrimination against individuals with disabilities in all areas of public life, including jobs, schools, transportation, and all public and private places that are open to the general public.

Passage of the ADA was a landmark achievement, but of course, it did not end all discrimination against people with disabilities. It prohibits discrimination based on physical or mental disability, and it increases access to employment opportunities for organizations with fifteen or more employees. It mandates that new buildings be made accessible, but does not call for access for older buildings. It forbids discrimination in housing. Different provisions of the ADA are regulated by parts of the federal government, such as the Department of Justice, Equal Employment Opportunity Commission, and Federal Communications Commission.[45]

Current and Future Challenges

Today we see the extreme wealth gap, the drive for ever-greater profits, and the corresponding inadequate government funding for basic needs. Just as Richard Nixon first vetoed the Rehabilitation Act in the early 1970s, citing its cost, politicians today call for austerity and insist there is no money for social programs. So despite the passage of important laws, many people with disabilities are still locked out of society and barred from participation.

In addition, rapid changes in late-stage capitalism have created for the working class as a whole similar challenges people with disabilities have been facing for a long time. Workers, whether disabled or not, must labor for capitalists to sustain themselves. As the rich have grown richer, the real value of wages has fallen for those whose work made them rich. Poverty, hunger, and homelessness are on the rise. The struggles people with disabilities have fought for are connected to all worker struggles: universal health care, affordable housing and education, and a job at a livable wage with safe working conditions.

SSI: Inadequate for Sustaining Life

Supplemental Security Income (SSI), a government program created to provide financial support for the elderly and disabled who cannot meet their basic needs on their own, forces disabled individuals across the country to live in poverty due to restrictive conditions and inadequate funding.

The issue affects those who fear for their future, asking: How will I support myself? Can I meet my own needs? The SSI program doesn't provide enough assistance for its recipients actually to meet their needs. Benefits sit significantly below the poverty line. An SSI recipient cannot have more than $2,000 in assets at any time. This means that recipients can't save for emergencies, or they risk losing all their benefits. A disabled person who chooses to get married may lose their benefits entirely. As a result, disabled individuals still do not have marriage equality.

Impact of COVID-19 Pandemic on People with Disabilities

Because the limited public health system is severely underfunded, the COVID-19 pandemic has been particularly devastating in the US. People with disabilities always face additional challenges under capitalism, and they can be even more vulnerable during emergencies, such as pandemics. For example, government statistics have shown the deadly impact COVID-19 has had on patients who need regular dialysis. In 2020, there were eighteen thousand additional deaths of people who received dialysis treatment compared to the year before. Many did not have COVID-19, but they were unable to receive consistent life-saving treatment because the country was unprepared for the pandemic's chaotic impact.[46]

Alice Wong, the founder of the Disability Visibility Project which collects oral histories of Americans with disabilities in conjunction with StoryCorps, has spoken and written about how COVID-19 has disrupted lives, intensifying challenges that disabled people have always had to live with.[47] In an interview, Wong made some striking points about the pandemic and ableism:

> Disabled people have always lived on the margins. And people on the margins really notice what's going on, having to navigate through systems and institutions, not being understood. When the pandemic first hit, the public was up in arms about adjusting to life at home—isolation and lack of access. These are things that many disabled and chronically ill people have experienced. Disabled people have been trying forever to advocate for online learning, for accommodations in the workplace. The response was: "Oh, we don't have the resources," "It's just not possible." But with the majority inconvenienced, it happened. Suddenly people actually had to think about access and flexibility. That is ableism, where you don't think disabled people exist, you don't think sick people exist.

Wong pointed to ableism "in the way our leaders talk about the risks, the mortality, about people with severe illnesses as if they're a write-off. I am so tired of having to assert myself. What kind of world is this where we have to defend our humanity? What is valued in our society?" She called ableism "an ideology, just like white supremacy."[48]

Honoring Militant Leaders in the Struggle

Despite the passage of the ADA and other victories born in struggle, being disabled can still be a life-and-death matter under capitalism. The drive for profits led to the deaths of two significant leaders in the struggle. Their situations are shared by many.

Carrie Ann Lucas

On February 24, 2019, at the age of forty-seven, Carrie Ann Lucas, a disability rights lawyer, advocate, and activist for disabled parents, died. Lucas was the founder of Disabled Parents' Rights, a nonprofit organization that fought for the rights of disabled people to have and raise children; she adopted four children with disabilities. She was also a professor and photographer, and was involved in connecting many civil rights issues, advocating for the inclusion of voices of people of color and LGBTQ people in the disability arena. Her death was the result of the profit-motivated health-care system and its cutbacks.

Always a militant, Lucas and nine others with disabilities were arrested after a fifty-eight-hour sit-in at the Denver office of Senator Cory Gardner in 2017, when ADAPT demonstrated against Medicaid budget cuts. When she was arrested, Lucas turned off her power chair and resisted arrest by refusing to tell police how to turn it on.

Lucas, who had a rare form of muscular dystrophy, used a power wheelchair and a ventilator. She also had low vision, was hard of hearing, and had type 1 diabetes. According to her Facebook page, "an arbitrary denial from an insurance company caused a plethora of health problems, exacerbating her disabilities and eventually leading to her premature death."[49]

In January 2018, she got a cold which turned into a lung infection. UnitedHealthcare refused to pay for the specific inhaled antibiotic she needed, instead forcing her to take a less effective drug. Her severe reaction to the medication led to a rapid decline in her health, which included affecting her ability to speak and her death a year later from septic shock. Ironically, UnitedHealthcare's attempt to save $2,000 ultimately cost over $1 million in health care costs.[50]

Engracia Figueroa

On October 31, 2021, disability activist Engracia Figueroa died from complications from a skin ulcer (common amongst people with paralysis) that she developed after United Airlines destroyed her $30,000 wheelchair—which is the average cost of a motorized chair. She was fifty-one years old.

Figueroa was a member of Hand in Hand, an organization that advocates for better conditions for domestic workers, including nannies and homecare attendants.[51] Hand in Hand called her a "joyful, fierce, creative leader."[52] Figueroa was also the President of the Board of Communities Actively Living Independent and Free, an independent living center in Los Angeles, an actor, animal rights activist, and surfer.[53]

In July 2019, she traveled to the Care Can't Wait rally in Washington, DC, representing Hand in Hand, to demand that Congress allocate more money for health care. On the way back, the airline destroyed her wheelchair, which was critical to her independence, as well as essential to maintaining her health.

"It was like my worst nightmare came true. My wheelchair is custom-made for me and my spinal cord injury. It's a $30,000 machine that is not easy to replace, and without it, I am now stuck at home," Figueroa said in a press release at the time.[54]

This is fairly common. In 2021, at least 7,239 wheelchairs or scooters were lost, damaged, delayed, or stolen on the country's largest airlines, according to the Air Travel Consumer Report.[55] That's about twenty per day. Many chairs are custom designed to fit the user's body to prevent pressure sores. Without this specific chair, the potential for a life-threatening infection is increased.[56]

Figueroa was stuck in the airport for nearly five hours, forced to sit in a broken manual wheelchair. Her struggle to maintain her balance over that time in the faulty device led to the development of a pressure sore. When she was finally able to return home, she experienced acute pain and was admitted to the hospital shortly after. Instead of replacing the demolished wheelchair, United Airlines insisted that they would only pay to repair it. But a motorized wheelchair that has undergone that much damage poses a severe fire risk and is unsafe.

Figueroa waged a struggle against United and eventually got them to replace her original chair. But months in an inadequate replacement chair provided by the airline worsened her pressure sore causing muscle spasms, severe edema, an inability to eat, and two additional hospitalizations. The sore became infected, and the infection eventually reached her hip bone, requiring emergency surgery to remove the infected bone and tissue, and causing her death on October 31.

While Figueroa was dying in the hospital, she is said to have been pushing to keep "disability rights at the forefront," according to her friend and fellow advocate Madelaine Reis.[57]

She tweeted, "Linking the disabled rights movement to Black Lives Matter and other oppressed groups to build solidarity."

"I would tell people to continue to fight ableism and understand the importance of disability rights. Wheelchairs are an extension of someone's body, and disabled lives like hers matter," Reis said.[58]

The death of these two activists who contributed so much is a blow not just to the disability rights movement, but to all progressive humanity. The most bitter part is that they did not have to die. Figueroa and Lucas, so familiar with the ins and outs of getting resources that they were actually advocates for others, could not save their own lives because the fundamental fault lies in the system itself.

Their needless deaths show that, while the struggle for lifesaving reforms is important, they are always under threat under capitalism. Building a society where all people can flourish means organizing to eliminate the capitalist system. This system simply does not value the lives of any of us, whether with disabilities or not.

BUILDING SOLIDARITY BETWEEN CARE WORKERS AND CLIENTS

I am fifty-seven years old. My diagnosis is incomplete quadriplegia. I was sick for ten years before I was properly diagnosed. I saw many doctors over that ten-year period from 2007 to 2016. They gave me all kinds of diagnoses, like altitude sickness and osteonecrosis. One doctor said we should wait at least six months and just see what happens. Within a year of that interaction, I started using a wheelchair. None of the doctors diagnosed a spinal cord injury, which, according to my surgeon, was caused by bone spurs pressing down on my cervical spinal cord. These bone spurs were likely caused by trauma which could have been related to a minor accident, sports, or almost anything.

During this time, I was largely unemployed, having previously worked as a public health professional. To make ends meet, I worked manual jobs like pizza delivery, masonry, carpet cleaning, and house cleaning. I didn't have access to health care. Before my health issues, I had been very physically active, but now while working these types of jobs, I was in a lot of physical pain and came home exhausted, and the pain kept on increasing. On February 11, 2017, I applied for disability benefits.

I applied for in-home support services eight times and was denied each time. My mom, my dad, my comrade, my social worker, and a community advocate all came to my appeal for services. Everyone was in shock that I was being denied. They kept on asking: How is it that they are denying you services?

Author John Daly engages a caregiver in political discussion. Photo: Liberation News

The biggest delay was caused by one piece of paper that had been misfiled. The lost document was finally found at the insistence of my mother. She called the Office of Long Term Care at the federal Department of Human Services repeatedly, developing a relationship with the worker who answered the phone—this worker also happened to be disabled. Eventually, the worker tracked down the document that had been misfiled. That's how I started getting thirty hours of service a week in January 2019, nearly two years after my initial application.

Before that, it was family, friends, neighbors, strangers, ex-prisoners, and other poor people who helped me. One neighbor would always check to make sure I had eaten breakfast. Another one of my neighbors in North Baton Rouge, Louisiana, would always come into my apartment, empty the urinals first, and then make me coffee. I was so embarrassed that she had to do that. At the same time, it tells you something about our class, that people would reach out to help a man they barely knew. This is why socialist ideas make so much sense to workers when explained—it's about putting human needs first and taking care of the entire community. People can relate to that.

Conditions for Care Workers

Being approved for a set number of hours of care a week, however, does not mean my life is now a utopia. The way the home health assistance system works leads to inadequate support for people with disabilities and extreme poverty for the workers. The workers who come to help me live in poverty. I think most are making less than what I make on disability, and I don't make anything near the top. They often come to work hungry. In the deep South where I live, it seems like home assistance is a cheap makeover of the Jim Crow domestic work system portrayed in the movie *The Help*.

There are 2.4 million home care workers in the US. This job is expected to grow more than any other in the country in the coming period as the number of retirees increases, with 21 percent of the population predicted to be at retirement age in 2030. Yet caring for people in the home is one of the poorest paid jobs. Close to one in five aides live below the poverty line.[59]

Home health aides, home attendants, and personal aides help their clients with activities of daily life, including shopping for food and necessities, cooking, light housekeeping, laundry, and bathing. But this can vary greatly depending on the needs of the client. Cooking often means learning the special dietary needs of the homebound person and preparing their food accordingly. It can also mean cutting someone's food or feeding someone who can't feed themselves. Assistance may need to be hands-on. Bathing can mean fully bathing a person, head to toe, and dressing and undressing them. Many clients need to be lifted or lowered into wheelchairs or on and off commodes; others are incontinent and need diapers changed. Still, others must have their positions rotated in bed every few hours to prevent pressure sores. Dementia patients need constant attention.

At the same time, many home care providers are expected to assist clients in taking medication, making sure they take them on time, be familiar with any medical equipment the client uses or needs, teach them self-care skills, make doctor appointments and escort patients to these appointments, or monitor medical conditions and report them to a visiting nurse.[60]

To pay the average rent in a US city, a care worker must take on two clients and work sixty to eighty hours a week. They could end up being clients themselves due to the backbreaking labor they do. And in fact, some people who have disabilities themselves end up becoming caregivers because they cannot otherwise survive.

During the pandemic, home health aides were extremely vulnerable to contracting and dying from COVID-19 as a result of inadequate personal protective equipment, as well as a lack of sick days and few, if any, health benefits.[61]

In Louisiana, workers can be called at the last minute and be expected to show up to work. They pay for their gas, drive their own cars, and need to fill out elaborate federal forms on top of actually doing the job, ultimately receiving pay that is barely above the federal minimum wage. Before the COVID-19 pandemic, Louisiana caregivers started at $7.35 per hour, during the pandemic, pay went up to $9 per hour.[62]

Without a union, these workers have almost no rights. They are subcontractors of outside contractors and other subcontractors. This system is supposed to be monitored by the state, which has very little power since the care of 69 percent of Medicaid recipients is managed by private insurance companies that prioritize high profits for stockholders and not the quality of life for clients.[63]

The workers need to drive to my home. How do you maintain a car in the United States, earning $9 an hour when gas is over $3 a gallon? Care workers don't get paid days off, and if their kids get sick, they don't have insurance, and they're not supposed to take time off to take them to the doctor.

In Louisiana, these workers often are not certified, and yet they have to know how to deal with all different types of disabilities and all types of medical equipment. And in my case, they have to assist me in interacting with the community. How do you do that during a pandemic? They must understand things that neurologists, psychiatrists, social workers, and many other professionals may not fully understand.

The extreme poverty and oppression of caregivers make it hard for them to maintain continuity in their jobs. Care workers may be impacted by systemic racism, housing instability, lack of reliable transportation, the need to care for their relatives, lack of childcare, immigration issues, or family members caught in the prison industrial complex.

Continuity is critical to developing routines and personal relationships. For the client, each new caregiver is a new relationship, a new person who needs to learn where things are located and how tasks need to be done. This can be exhausting and frustrating for the person who needs the help.

Union Organizing among Home Health Aides and Caregivers

Improving the pay and working conditions of home care workers can only improve the quality of care for disabled people who need these services to live independently and with dignity. The best way for working people in a capitalist society to improve their conditions of work is to join a union and engage in collective bargaining.

In-home caregiving work has historically fallen into the category of domestic work. The National Labor Relations Act (NLRA) of 1935, which gave US workers the right to organize, support and join a union without being fired, along with other labor protections of the time, but excluded domestic workers and agricultural workers. While both Black and white workers were excluded, this was seen as a capitulation to racist bosses because, at the time, 65 percent of the entire African American workforce was engaged in domestic or agricultural work, with an even greater percentage in the South.[64]

Despite this legal obstacle to organizing among domestic workers, there have been important efforts to organize domestic workers in the South, most notably those first conducted by communists as described in the classic history of communism in Alabama, Robin Kelley's *Hammer and Hoe*. The Great Depression set the stage for the struggles described here. The worsening economic situation in the US today draws us to look even more closely at past struggles like the Communist Party USA (CPUSA) organizing in Alabama.

In 1920, Black women comprised 60 percent of Birmingham's 20,082 female workers, and 87 percent were "engaged in domestic work," according to Kelley.[65]

Black female domestics experienced layoffs, speedups (employers used the threat of competition to extract more work over less time), and wage cuts because of overall cutbacks in the use of paid household labor and the increasing utilization of labor-saving devices. Without the benefit of sick pay, vacations, or regular hours, some women toiled in white kitchens for as low as $1.50 to $2.00 per week. Wages were so low during the 1930s that many women earned just enough to pay their rent and lived day-to-day on the food they "toted" from their employer's kitchen. According to the 1930 Census, approximately 82 percent of, or sixteen thousand, black female wage earners were engaged in domestic services, and in 1935, at least eight thousand black female domestic workers had registered with the Alabama Employment Service.[66]

The CPUSA failed to organize Southern domestic workers at a large scale in the 1930s, but we should still study their experiences and understand why they could even get started. Communist organizers understood the working situation of Black women domestic workers as being one part of their overall life experience as Black people, as women, and as workers in a capitalist system. The approach to organizing these workers didn't simply agitate around work conditions but incorporated community struggles against evictions, for unemployment relief, against racism, and police brutality. Today, we see renewed efforts to organize care workers in the South and a recent history of success in organizing care workers on the East and West Coasts by Service Workers International Union (SEIU) 1199.

Ongoing Struggles Today of Care Workers in the South

Organized labor-community initiatives like North Carolina's NC Raise Up and Fight for $15 have begun the nascent organizing. They have focused on 2021 promises from the Biden administration of pay increases, more benefits, and workplace protections for this sector of workers, promises which have yet to materialize.[67,68]

NC Raise Up and Fight for $15 initiated a petition in April 2021 advocating for higher wages. They called a town hall meeting in early June, and, later that month, a rally. They continue to organize and advocate to raise the state's minimum wage in North Carolina from $7.25 per hour to $15 per hour—providing a living wage for direct care workers for the elderly and disabled, food workers, and others.

On April 22, 2021, Chanelle Croxton, the North Carolina director of the National Domestic Workers Alliance, one of the organizations of the Raising Wages NC coalition, hosted a virtual press conference promoting House Bill 612 and its counterpart Senate Bill 723, which if passed, would guarantee a $15 per hour minimum wage for all workers in North Carolina. Among the speakers were two Black women who are care workers.[69]

"I get no health care benefits, no 401k, no paid sick days, and I haven't taken a vacation in five years," said Cummie Davis, an organizer with NC Rise Up and Fight for $15, speaking at the news conference. Davis is a Certified Nursing Assistant (CNA) who works two careworker jobs, one at an assisted living home and another as a home caregiver. She has suffered injuries from her physically intensive labor but cannot afford health care. Davis continued, "Workers like me have waited long enough, we need a raise right now!"[70]

Diondre Clark, a CNA and an organizer with the National Domestic Workers Alliance, works three careworker jobs to make ends meet. Clark said, "There's no way I could work just one job and survive . . . I like what I do, but it's taking a toll."[71]

"I've been a certified nursing assistant for twenty-eight years, but today I only earn $10 per hour as a home care worker," added Sandra Brown, a member of NC Raise Up/Fight for $15. Brown spoke to the crux of the crisis: "No wonder there's a growing shortage of home care workers in our country!"[72]

'Your Job Can Only Improve if You Do the Work and Organize'

SEIU 1199 has organized 125,000 home care workers, and seeks to organize more.[73] According to Michael Luciano, an administrative organizer with SEIU 1199, "There's never been a better time to do it than right now." He points out that in an industry with extremely high turnover and instability for the clients, unions have eliminated that high turnover in addition to significantly reducing injuries on the job.[74]

"I think the number one thing about union contracts that people really appreciate are guaranteed wage rates and guaranteed yearly increases" and paid time off, said Luciano. "The other really important thing about a union contract that isn't very sexy is a grievance procedure—being able to formally fight back against an unjust termination or an unjust discipline," explained Luciano. The home care industry is rife with retaliation and punitive action against the clients and the workers in situations where a grievance procedure or even a simple mediation would suffice to resolve the issue. How would an organized caregiver workforce benefit clients with disabilities? "One of the most desirable things from a client's perspective is stability, having the same person," Luciano adds.

Another thing is making the employer pay for training and supervision. "These companies hire anyone for your job with little to no training; there's no supervision. In the end, the clients are left without the assistance they need."

"Both the worker and the client are oppressed by the same system," this organizer explained. "Workers organizing a union not only improve conditions for themselves but make it better for the clients as well."

Obstacles to Organizing and an Alternative Organizing Approach

There are about sixty-five thousand home care agencies in the country.[75] In the South, unions may find it difficult to organize the many small home care agencies that contract with larger agencies that contract with the federal government. But the agricultural workers in the Florida-based Immokalee Coalition of Workers (ICW) and their strategy of organizing a community coalition and targeting buyers may point the way for progress in winning gains for home care workers.[76] Agricultural workers, like domestic workers, are not protected by the NLRA.

The Immokalee farm workers pick tomatoes on many different farms. Instead of negotiating with each individual farm owner for better working conditions and higher salaries, the coalition representing the workers went to the buyers of the tomatoes, like Taco Bell, Wendy's, and ARAMARK, to pressure them to buy tomatoes only from the farms that meet ICW demands. These include paying the workers one penny more a pound for the tomatoes they pick, which would bring their wages up to $15 per hour. It includes conforming to a worker-determined standard for decent and safe working conditions and their Fair Food Program.[77] Students got involved and the community brought pressure through marches, petitions, and boycotts.

If this model were applied to home care workers, pressure would be brought on the main buyer of their services, Medicaid, which is the ultimate decision maker about reimbursements and wages. So we could build a coalition of disabled people and caregivers together, plus the labor movement at large, to put pressure on Medicaid to raise wages, to improve the working conditions of caregivers, and thus improve the living conditions of the people they serve. Higher wages and benefits, and established and enforceable work standards, would bring more people into the field with higher minimum standards of training, and the potential for more consistency and continuity of providers, leading to improved care for the people they assist.

Prospects for Unity and Struggle: John's Perspective

The first month I received services in 2019, I met with the local Department of Health and asked when the workers would get a raise. I told them, "There's no way disabled people can have dignity if our caregivers don't have it."

How can we build maximum unity between those who struggle with disabilities and the workers who can help us fulfill our need for independence? There can understandably be animosity between care workers and clients. The way home care services are now delivered places so much stress on both the workers and the clients that it may appear that the problem is between them when it's not.

On the surface, it might seem like there is a contradiction between the interests of the clients and the workers. The person with a disability is struggling for more hours of care, more care, and more highly qualified workers, while the worker is trying not to work to exhaustion, to be able to get to work when poverty causes them so many problems that they must deal with at home.

As a client, I sometimes feel like I'm a set of hours to the workers. But before I became disabled, I was a worker, so I understand that "this many hours equals that many dollars" and that's how much they have. But seeing other people as hours and dollars is not something that workers or disabled people came up with ourselves; it is something the system put on us.

There are many shared concerns. Many of the workers also have disabilities. Of course, they would after working twelve-hour shifts, cooking and cleaning and picking up heavy things all the time, and then going home and doing the same thing. Deep down, the clients often understand this even when they might not show it. That's because they're struggling too, and they may be calling out the only person they see: the worker who appeared at the front door that day.

The objective conditions exist for workers and clients to understand each others' struggles. Teachers' unions say, "the working conditions of teachers are the learning conditions of students." This fundamental fact underlies a unified struggle to improve education for children and improve the experience and compensation of teachers. It resolves the seeming contradiction between teachers and students. Likewise, the working conditions of caregivers are the living conditions of people with disabilities. This fact lays the basis for a joint struggle.

These care workers are disabled people's lifeline. There should be a section in the local news about them. Why don't we have celebrations and parades for the people who help others? And more importantly, decent wages and benefits?

We can break free together because solidarity is where the solution lies.

KILLER AND DISABLER OF MILLIONS

- A Laotian child's legs are shattered when she triggers a landmine airdropped into fields fifty years ago.
- Elderly military veterans mourn a fallen comrade, poisoned by Agent Orange in Vietnam and living in pain since the 1970s.
- Children today are born with birth defects in Vietnam, Laos, Cambodia, and Iraq long after those wars ended. In the US, similar cases are traced to fathers who fought in those distant wars.
- Younger veterans, poisoned by burn-pit fumes in Iraq in the 1990s, fight a military bureaucracy that refuses to acknowledge their debilitating illnesses or their cause.
- A whole community in Hawaii suffers severe headaches, rashes, hair loss, mental fog, menstrual abnormalities, and other symptoms when a naval base leaks fuel into their water supply.
- A homeless veteran, suffering traumatic brain injury and debilitating post-traumatic stress, shaken by memories of all he has seen and done, commits suicide.

What does all this suffering have in common? It was caused by the US military, the global enforcement arm of the capitalist empire.

The US military disables people around the world. The global victims of US military violence and the soldiers share a common bond:

both groups are victimized and seen as expendable by the profit-driven capitalist war machine. This chapter will give an overview of how the US war machine created and continues to create disabilities.

Hiroshima and Nagasaki

The US is the only country ever to use nuclear weapons, and its targets were civilian populations. In 1945, the Pentagon dropped atomic bombs on the Japanese cities of Hiroshima and Nagasaki. Hundreds of thousands of women, men, and children died in the first six months after the bombing.[78] The bombings condemned hundreds of thousands of survivors to a life-long struggle with multiple cancers caused by radiation poisoning.

Agent Orange

Today, 4.8 million Vietnamese people across three generations suffer from the effects of toxic herbicides used as defoliants by the US in the decade-long Vietnam War. They suffer from cancers, physical deformities, and other chronic physical and neurological ailments.[79] Although fifteen different herbicides were sprayed over Vietnam between 1961 and 1971, they came to be collectively labeled as Agent Orange. One of them, Dioxin, is among the most toxic substances on earth. The military sprayed eleven million gallons of Agent Orange in Vietnam. An additional estimated 475,500 gallons were sprayed in Laos and 40,900 in Cambodia.

The massive spraying in Vietnam was done to defoliate areas that might conceal Vietnamese fighters and to destroy crops grown by villagers that might be used to feed fighters. With their crops destroyed, rural populations were displaced, forced into refugee camps, or fled to the cities. Agent Orange has also contaminated soil and groundwater in Vietnam.[80]

The impact on Vietnamese people and US service members has been devastating. Generations of children have been born with birth defects, both in Vietnam and the US. The survivors and descendents of the survivors of this genocidal military tactic struggle to function in their daily lives as a result of illnesses and injuries caused by Agent Orange.

Although many people in the US know it as "the Vietnam War," Cambodia and Laos were also victims of US aggression. While having given some recognition and money to Vietnam for poisoning its land

and people with Agent Orange,[81] Washington has not done so with Laos or Cambodia.[82] In these countries, as in Vietnam, the grandchildren of those heavily exposed to Agent Orange are born without eyes, or with shortened limbs, hip dysplasia, clubbed feet, and other disabling conditions.[83]

US Soldiers Also Poisoned

US soldiers were also exposed to Agent Orange in Vietnam, poisoned by it, and have had children with severe birth defects due to their parents' exposure. The North Dakota State Department has stated that approximately three hundred thousand Vietnam veterans have died as a result of exposure to Agent Orange, five times the fifty-eight thousand US soldiers killed in the Vietnam War.[84]

The organization Veterans for Peace (VFP) has initiated the Vietnam Agent Orange Relief and Responsibility Campaign to fight for justice and compensation for all victims of Agent Orange, in both Vietnam and the US.[85] VFP supported a class action lawsuit by the Vietnam Association for Victims of Agent Orange/Dioxin against the US chemical companies that made the defoliant. A judge dismissed the suit in US federal court. The Vietnamese government filed suit in US court against Dow Chemical Co., Monsanto Co., and thirty other producers of these toxic chemicals charging they caused cancer and birth defects, only to have the suit dismissed.[86] Only in the last two decades has the US government taken any responsibility for the poisonings and committed money for care, though most feel it is too little too late. VFP is now working on passage of legislation to accomplish this, the HR 3518, Victims of Agent Orange Relief Act of 2021.[87]

Landmines and Unexploded Ordnance—the Remnants of War

People in Vietnam, Laos, and Cambodia also suffer from the massive deployment of US landmines and bombs in the 1960s and 1970s to this day, which still kill and wound victims. For example, Vietnam is today saturated with an estimated eight hundred thousand tons of unexploded bombs dropped there by the US, according to the Mines Advisory Group, an international organization working to reduce risks by removing landmines and other deadly ordnances. These bombs continue to kill and maim long after hostilities have ended.[88]

A school in central Vietnam. The sign warns students to stay on marked paths to avoid live land mines left by the US. Photo: Joyce Chediac

Unexploded landmines, embedded in almost seventy countries around the globe, kill or maim fifteen to twenty thousand people each year, according to estimates by the International Campaign to Ban Landmines. Civilians, many women and children, account for more than 80 percent of the victims. As a result of US aggression, Vietnam, Laos, Iraq, and Afghanistan are some of the most heavily landmined countries in the world.[89]

Landmines are incredibly cheap to produce, costing as little as $3 per mine, but finding and destroying just one single mine costs between $300 and $1,000, placing a considerable burden for their removal on governments already devastated by war. Joint efforts to remove mines between former US soldiers and the people whose land still has minefields are building anti-imperialist solidarity. For example, Veterans for Peace is demanding that the United States, "sign the Landmine Ban Treaty, support the Convention on Cluster Munitions and congressional efforts to end the use of cluster bombs, give assistance to the victims of the explosive remnants of war, and educate others about this horrific legacy of war."[90]

Depleted Uranium Poisoning

Depleted uranium (DU), a chemically toxic and radioactive waste product of the nuclear industry, is used in bullets in armor-piercing weapons and as armor for some tanks. It has been linked to increased cancers and birth defects for soldiers and civilians who come in contact with it. Like Agent Orange, it causes long-term environmental contamination.

DU weapons were used extensively by the US military in Iraq in two wars there, in 1991 and 2003. In 2003, during the second war on Iraq, the Pentagon broke its own rules limiting the use of these weapons to be used only against tanks and armored vehicles, firing depleted uranium weapons in many civilian areas.[91] The Pentagon also confirmed that it had used them most recently in Syria.[92]

The city of Fallujah in Iraq was hit particularly hard and has suffered significantly increased rates of cancer and birth defects in years after the initial devastating assault. In a 2013 interview with BBC, Samira Alaana, a pediatrician at Fallujah General Hospital, noticed a wide range of birth defects after the US began its second war and occupation of Iraq in 2003. She stated:

> We began logging these cases in October 2009, and we have determined that 144 babies are born with a deformity for every thousand live births. We believe it has to be related to contamination caused by the fighting in our city, even now, nearly ten years later. It is not unique to Fallujah; hospitals throughout the Anbar Governorate and many other regions of Iraq are recording spiraling increases.[93]

One study showed that children born with birth defects had approximately three times the lead levels and six times the mercury levels compared to children born in neighboring Iran, which was not suffering US military attack. High levels of lead and mercury are associated with physical, neurological, and cognitive developmental challenges, with lifelong impacts on the ability to function of the people exposed.

US military veterans and Iraqis have been disabled due to these wars, and neither group has received the acknowledgment and support they deserve. Burn pits, in which toxic wastes are destroyed, were used by the US military, mainly in Iraq and Afghanistan. The unregulated burning process emits toxic substances and carcinogens, which have been singled out as a significant source of contamination of US soldiers and civilians living near the pits.[94] This environmental devastation and the threat of disabling toxicity remain long after the military leaves.[95]

Post-Traumatic Stress and Traumatic Brain Injury

Post-traumatic stress, a debilitating mental health condition caused by exposure to intense trauma, can develop years after the initial trauma and linger for many after. It has long been associated with military service. When veterans returned from World War I where they were exposed to the horrors of modern warfare, they experienced what was known as "shell shock," now called post-traumatic stress disorder (PTSD). Recently another term has emerged, post-traumatic stress injury (PTSI), with "injury" as a possibly more accurate descriptor.

Regarded as an unwillingness to fight, cowardness, a character flaw, or a moral failing in the World War I period, troops exhibiting PTSD were often treated harshly. This take on post-traumatic stress was dominant through World War II. Viewing it as a disorder or injury in need of treatment comes out of the movement in opposition to the Vietnam War.

The concept that the Vietnam War "exacted a form of psychic damage on American soldiers" originated with the anti-war activists of Vietnam Veterans Against the War (VVAW) and psychiatrists Chaim Shatan and Robert Jay Lifton, who worked with the anti-war veterans. "Post-Vietnam Syndrome," Shatan wrote, was caused by the "unconsummated grief" of a "brutal and brutalizing war."[96]

VVAW organized "rap sessions" during which many returning soldiers traced their intense anxiety, battle dreams, explosively aggressive, self-destructive, and other behaviors to the contradiction between what the US government had told them about that war, and the reality of what they saw and were expected to do on the ground.[97] VVAW's advocacy was instrumental in securing official recognition for this condition. The diagnosis has since been refined and extended to civilians as well.[98]

Some 30 percent of Vietnam War veterans have suffered from some sort of PTSD in their lifetimes, according to the Veterans Administration. But post-traumatic stress is not limited to Vietnam veterans. It is found in US veterans who served in Iraq and Afghanistan. The US Department of Veterans Affairs National Center for PTSD estimates that 11 to 20 percent of US veterans who served in wars in the Middle East suffer from PTSD in a given year.[99]

Even drone operators, deploying killing technology far from the war, can suffer post-traumatic stress. Daniel Hale is an Air Force drone operator imprisoned for forty-five months in 2021 for leaking secret documents exposing the widespread killing of civilians by US drones.[100] Hale wrote a letter to the judge who sentenced him. He described watching civilians at a peaceful gathering, knowing he would soon watch a missile kill them, and the trauma of witnessing "scenes of graphic violence carried out from the cold comfort of a computer chair."[101]

Traumatic brain injuries (TBI) are caused most frequently in the military by bullet penetration, violent impact, and especially by shock waves from explosive weapons. There is a range of mild to extreme symptoms for this condition, such as persistent headaches, physical and mental fatigue, dizziness, blurred vision, memory problems, difficulty sleeping, nausea, convulsions, and more. Symptoms can be neurological or mental-health-related. More than 430,000 US military service members were diagnosed with TBI between 2000 and 2020.[102]

US veterans were sent to war but often abandoned with little more than a "thank you for your service" when they returned.[103] Their status today shows they are not getting the mental health and other support they need. For example, from 2008–2017, more US veterans committed suicide (sixty thousand) than were killed in the Vietnam War (fifty-eight thousand).[104] Untreated PTSD and TBI can also send veterans on a downward spiral that puts them at high risk of losing their homes.[105]

While only eight percent of the population has served in US wars, 17 percent of the homeless population are veterans.[106] Approximately 53 percent of homeless veterans suffer from a disability. Concern and improved treatment for US military veterans is important and should be supported.

Military Bases

The US has nearly eight hundred military bases spread around the globe with toxic munitions and fuel storage tanks that can destroy the environment and kill or disable service members, their families, and people living nearby. The military rarely monitors these toxic substances, and environmental poisoning from US bases is common.[107]

Vieques, Puerto Rico

The US Navy used the island of Vieques, part of Puerto Rico, as a target for bombing practice and as a weapons testing site from the 1940s until the island's people forced the Navy to leave in 2003. In the 1940s, the US Navy "purchased" 60 percent of the island and forced many families and farmers out of their homes, out of work, and off their island. The struggle to regain control of their island by the nine thousand inhabitants was led by the fisherman of the community, which culminated with a victory in 2003.

While the Navy left the island, it left behind the clean-up of the toxic damage from using napalm, depleted uranium, and other heavy metals from the thousands of bombing runs it conducted. In 1998, the US Navy dropped twenty-three thousand bombs on the island.

The consequences of the poisoning of the island and the waters around it are typical of the damage caused by the US military. According to a report by the North American Congress on Latin America:

> Dangerous levels of cadmium and lead appear in the island's crabs. Lead is concentrated in pasture grass grazed by horses and cattle. Ordnance occasionally washes ashore. Such contamination from heavy metals and other toxins poses major environmental and health concerns. For example, the island's cancer rate is 27 percent higher than the rest of Puerto Rico, raising troubling questions about the military's toxic legacy and its short- and long-term impact on islanders' health.[108]

Oahu, Hawaii and Red Hill Fuel Contamination

Hawaii's Joint Base Pearl Harbor-Hickam is a site of an ongoing crisis as tens of thousands of gallons have leaked from fuel tanks at its Red Hill fuel storage facility into the aquifer that supplies water to the base and surrounding community on the island of Oahu.

The storage facility, built following Japan's 1941 attack on Pearl Harbor, is made of twenty underground steel fuel tanks that are known to be corroding, each one approximately 250 feet tall. The entire system, which can hold about 250 million gallons of fuel, sits approximately one hundred feet above the aquifer. There have been

More than five hundred protesters march on Oahu, Hawaii after the US Navy poisoned drinking water for thousands. Photo: J. Matt

several significant leaks of thousands of gallons into the water supply over the decades.[109]

In October 2021, the Hawaiian government fined the Navy $325,000 for violating environmental inspection regulations in 2020. In December of 2021, Hawaii state health officials announced that levels of gasoline-fuel hydrocarbons in the Navy's water system were up to 350 times higher than state standards for safe drinking water. The Navy has received heavy criticism from the Hawaiian government and the local community for withholding information about the extent of the problem.[110]

About ninety thousand people in the region use the Navy's contaminated water system. The Navy relocated about 3,500 military families into nearby hotels off the base.[111] People in the outlying community were left to fend for themselves. Toxins found in the water system include benzene, a known carcinogen. Because long-term exposure to toxins such as petroleum can lead to severe neurological damage, the crisis in Hawaii is not unique. In 2016, residents learned that the US Kadena Air Base in Okinawa, Japan, had contaminated the water supply of 450,000 Okinawans with per- and polyfluoroalkyl substances (PFAS), the "forever chemical" that does not decompose. It is estimated that the contaminants will affect Okinawa's water for generations.[112] There have been multiple releases into the surrounding community, and military officials have stonewalled efforts to address the problem.[113]

A 2017 article by the Center for Public Integrity noted: "At 149 current and former US military bases, the contamination is so severe that they have been designated Superfund sites by the US Environmental Protection Agency, meaning they are among the most hazardous areas in the country requiring cleanup."[114]

Environmental damage at military bases around the world, coupled with the government's secrecy, is a ticking time bomb threatening to cause death and disabilities well into the future.[115] The ever-increasing US military budget for bombing and maiming people abroad, while treating US soldiers' injuries as collateral damage, takes money away from much-needed medical and social services for people with disabilities, civilians, and veterans alike.

THE STATUS OF RIGHTS FOR PEOPLE WITH DISABILITIES

The Americans with Disabilities Act (ADA) was passed in Washington in 1990 before three thousand jubilant people with disabilities, many of whom fought fiercely for years for that legislation.[116] The law banned discrimination based on disability in employment, public accommodations, public services, transportation, and telecommunication. It was hailed as a milestone—the world's first declaration of equality[117] for people with disabilities. It became the model for the 2006 UN Convention on the Rights of Persons with Disabilities, which sets standards for eliminating social and physical obstacles for people with disabilities worldwide.[118]

The United States, the richest country in the world, certainly hasn't lacked the means to implement this act. How have disability rights fared since the ADA became law?

Today, the majority of people with disabilities still struggle to find jobs,[119] with fewer employed than in 1990. When they do work, they often earn less than non-disabled workers.[120] Most affordable housing is still not accessible, and people with disabilities face higher rates of housing insecurity.[121] People with disabilities also experience higher rates of food insecurity[122] and much higher rates of poverty than the overall population. They are overrepresented among the homeless and in prisons and jails. They struggle to get the health care they need.

While the ADA was the model for the UN Convention on the Rights of Persons with Disabilities, the US Congress never ratified this UN convention, which requires periodic inspections for compliance.

What Happened?

Although many gains were made initially, the concepts of disability inclusion, community support, and nondiscrimination were never made into the needed programs and supports to truly implement the ADA. The US government drifted back to its default: representing the capitalists, who see meeting the needs of people with disabilities as an added expense they don't want to incur.

Employers and landlords have ignored the laws, and government enforcement of the law has fallen far short. By 2020, thirty years[123] after the ADA's passage, violations abounded. As employers and landlords continue to disregard the laws, disability-related complaints remain the largest category filed with the federal agencies that enforce fair-housing and employment laws.

Advocates say that even though the ADA was passed, they still have to defend it. To push the ADA forward, they must navigate a host of bureaucratic mazes and/or fight all over again for implementation in state and local courts. They are up against conservative court decisions that have limited the ADA's efficacy and cut funds that could be used for implementation.

Discrimination Remains in Employment

In key areas, conditions have gone backward. Access to employment, one of the central elements of the ADA, is at an even lower level than before the ADA was passed. In 1990, 30 percent of people with disabilities were employed. By 2008, employment of people with disabilities stood at 23 percent. By 2012, twenty years after the ADA took effect, just 18 percent of working-age people with disabilities had jobs, compared to 64 percent of people without disabilities. In 2021, 19.1 percent of persons with a disability were working,[124] according to the US Bureau of Labor Statistics.

Workers with disabilities still face both explicit and implicit discrimination in the workplace, according to a recent University of Denver study.[125] When people with disabilities work, it is in lower-level positions where they work fewer hours and earn less money than people without disabilities.[126] While the ADA banned discrimination in employment, some employers, citing a 1938 law, have been permitted to apply for "special wage certificates" to pay their workers with disabilities far below minimum wage in "sheltered workshops." Meanwhile, the pittance provided by Social Security benefit programs, which many people with disabilities must rely upon to survive, have eligibility requirements that deter employment.

After decades of struggle for civil rights, capitalists continue to deny the jobs and resources to which people with disabilities are entitled, then reduce them to their disability and devalue them as "burdens on society."

Accessibility and Housing, Still Major Issues

Even though the Fair Housing Act[127] prohibits housing discrimination based on a disability, people with disabilities continue to face housing discrimination, making it harder to both obtain and maintain housing.[128]

Less than 5 percent[129] of housing in this country is accessible for people with moderate mobility difficulties, and less than 1 percent is accessible for wheelchair users.[130] With a national affordable housing shortage of more than seven million units,[131] even fewer housing units are accessible and affordable.

While the ADA resulted in tens of thousands of public spaces, buildings, and businesses being made accessible, along with transportation, accessibility is far from universal. Rural areas remain especially inaccessible. The political trend over the last thirty years of tax cuts for the rich and letting city infrastructures fall into disrepair has taken its toll on accessibility, especially in transportation.

For example, New York City is the center of world capitalism and the home of Wall Street. It is the richest city in the world,[132] home to 107 billionaires,[133] so it would seem the tax base is there to fund universal accessibility. Yet the city's subway system is still not accessible, and wheelchair users report chairlifts on the public buses are often broken. Sometimes they must wait while several buses with broken lifts pass until one arrives that can load their chairs, making travel unpredictable and exhausting.

Half of the Poor and a Quarter of the Homeless Have a Disability

Adults with disabilities experience poverty at more than twice the rate[134] of nondisabled adults; nearly half of adults[135] ages twenty-five to sixty-one who have lived in poverty for a year or more have a disability, and close to 25 percent[136] of the more than 580,000 people[137] who are homelessness on any given night in the United States have a disability. Women with disabilities[138] and disabled people of color[139] have even higher poverty rates.

The Fight for Health Care

Even when and if the existing laws are enforced, it is not enough to deal with the totalities of the lives of people with disabilities. The government needs to recognize and take responsibility for guaranteeing and implementing basic human rights to all working-class people: the right to a full and productive life, to health and medical care, to be free of hunger, to have adequate and safe shelter, to a job at decent pay, and to dignity and respect. These rights do not exist in the US.

According to a recent survey, people with disabilities identified health-care access as their most pressing problem. This includes getting better health-care access, getting a plan that will cover their needs, and even finding a doctor who is willing to treat them.[140]

It's no wonder, with the state of health care in the US. More than thirty million Americans have no health coverage. In addition, eleven state governments have refused to accept federal money to expand Medicaid insurance to their residents, deliberately leaving 3.7 million without insurance that would otherwise be covered.[141,142]

Medical bills are the number-one cause of personal bankruptcies in the US.[143] According to one study, 62.1 percent of bankruptcies were caused by medical issues.[144] Families that include people with disabilities hold higher amounts of medical debt[145] than the general population, and medical debt is a major cause of homelessness.

This is a result of the US government turning health care over to health management organizations, mega-hospitals, and giant pharmaceutical companies, which have jacked up the cost of health care and, at the same time, cut services in working-class areas where their profit rates are not as high as in affluent areas.

Public Hospitals Closed

In the thirty-two years since the ADA was passed, hospitals, modeling themselves on capitalist corporations, rapidly moved to prioritize profits and cost cutting above patient care and safety for health-care providers. From 1990 to 2005, with government and health profiteers working together, 40 public hospitals in cities were closed, and 156 others were converted to private ownership, leaving only half of the public hospitals open, according to National Nurses United (NNU), a union representing nurses. Between 2005 and now, 180 rural hospitals were closed, creating trauma deserts—no nearby ERs for emergency cases, says NNU.[146]

Fewer hospitals make health care an even scarcer commodity, allowing health-care corporations to increase prices. The result is skyrocketed profits. Hospitals, on average, charge $417 for every $100 in total costs, according to NNU.[147]

The cuts continue. As of this writing, major hospitals are cutting back on pediatric in-patient facilities and replacing them with adult ones, which are more profitable. They are doing this even as pediatric facilities are flooded with children suffering from respiratory syncytial virus.

In rural areas, where 20 percent of the US population lives, hospitals are facing additional cuts of $600 million in Medicare unless Congress renews funding. Local leaders call these cuts catastrophic, as they would leave whole areas without medical care. Many of these hospitals have already cut rural clinics.[148]

All of these cuts are especially devastating for people with disabilities who have less money than the population as a whole and who must now travel further for care.

Public Health Cuts Make Diabetes a National Epidemic

The least profitable area of health care is public health, the main agent for monitoring the health of a community and for bringing health education, self-help groups, and other elements of prevention to neighborhoods. At least thirty-eight thousand state and local public health jobs have disappeared since the 2008 recession, leaving a skeletal workforce.[149] This disregard for prevention both causes and worsens disability.

According to government figures, 34.3 million people, or 10.5 percent of the population, have diabetes, and one hundred thousand people died from that disease in 2021.[150] It is a national epidemic. Close to 17 percent of people with disabilities are diagnosed with diabetes.[151]

Untreated diabetes can lead to cardiovascular disease, liver malfunctioning, blindness, limb amputations, cognitive changes, and death. But this chronic disease is often preventable. Those at risk for developing type 2 diabetes can often be spotted through screening. Giving people access to health-care and health-promotion programs that provide education and support in making healthy lifestyle changes can go a long way to preventing or lessening the disease.[152] But the national public-health system that would take that on no longer exists. Additionally, there have been many scientific advances in care for those who have diabetes. But with thirty million people without any health-care coverage and others paying high insurance premiums before they can get care, these advances are not available to everyone.

So the disease advances. Diabetic amputations across the country grew by 50 percent between 2009 and 2015.[153] Annually, diabetics undergo 130,000 amputations, with the amputees often from low-income and underinsured neighborhoods. Black patients lose limbs at a rate triple that of others.[154] Shunning prevention, hospitals and other medical profiteers make thousands of dollars from amputations, with the chronically sick, the poor, and people of color suffering the worst consequences.[155]

By jacking up the price of insulin, giant pharmaceutical companies have done their part in the growth of this epidemic and the suffering, death, and disability it brings. Although it costs only $10 to produce a vial of insulin,[156] uninsured patients in the US pay $300 to $400 per vial of insulin because the three pharmaceutical corporations that control the nation's lucrative insulin market charge excessive prices with very little pushback from Congressional lawmakers.[157] This is a 1,100 percent increase since the 1990s when the ADA was passed.[158]

Some 14 percent of people[159] who use insulin in the US must spend at least 40 percent of their post-subsistence income—what is left after paying for food and housing—on insulin. So 1.3 million people in the US ration insulin due to high cost,[160] including an estimated one in four people with type 1 diabetes.[161] They are not alone. Nearly three in ten adults who take prescription drugs say that they have skipped doses, cut pills in half, or not filled prescriptions due to cost.[162] Many of these are people with disabilities.

The Fight to Be Seen by a Doctor

On top of all this, the drive for profits has diminished access to doctors for people with disabilities. People with disabilities have maintained for years that doctors do not treat them respectfully, medical offices aren't accessible, and health care for them is substandard. An October 2020 survey confirmed that all this was true—many doctors did not want to see people with disabilities and purposely sought to discourage them from being their patients.[163] This includes but is not limited to, people who ride wheelchairs.

Large medical and insurance institutions, for whom most doctors work, pressure their doctors to spend no more than fifteen minutes with each patient. These conglomerates aren't paying for accessible exam tables that can be dialed to different heights or scales that can accommodate wheelchairs. With financiers calling the shots, many doctors who think they can't complete a visit of a person with a disability within the allotted fifteen minutes have tried to get them out of their practice. Thus the survey found doctors are canceling appointments, telling people with disabilities that they could be served best elsewhere, or having their staff tell people with disabilities the doctor isn't taking appointments right now.

All this would seem criminal to anyone with a conscience. Yet government officials have looked the other way and even facilitated this selling of health care to the highest bidder, despite the blatant discrimination, pain, disability, and needless death that results. Policies and practices in the years that passed since the ADA became law reveal that the capitalist system has no intention of meeting the needs of people with disabilities.

A GLIMPSE INTO A LIBERATING FUTURE

The Soviet Union, the first socialist country, was birthed in 1917 from the ruins of World War I. It was immediately beset with civil war and besieged by imperialist armies. This left it with a very low economic and technical base to begin to meet human needs. Yet even during that time, the new socialist government took groundbreaking measures to empower and socially include people with disabilities.

The All-Russian Cooperative of Disabled People (VIKO), a national umbrella organization formed in 1921, was the first national pandisability advocacy organization in modern history. The All-Russian Union of the Blind was established in 1923. The All-Russian Union of the Deaf was established in 1926. These three organizations were controlled and operated by their disabled members with the support of and under the aegis of the national government. This was a first.

The Union of Soviet Socialist Republics (USSR) also became the first country in the world to establish a single and unified federal-level Office of Public Health in July 1918.[164]

It was one of the very first governments in the world to make the universal education of children with disabilities a national public policy. This effort was led by Lev S. Vygotsky.

Vygotsky was a brilliant scholar who supported the Russian revolutionary process and integrated Marxist and Leninist ideas into the developing field of psychology. As part of his theory of the sociocultural development of children, he understood "disability" dialectically as an interrelationship between the sociocultural environment and the unique characteristics of the individual. Much of his theorizing and research about teaching and learning, which are very influential today, focused on the education and empowerment of children with disabilities through the newly developing socialist education system. Vygotsky contracted tuberculosis in 1925 and conducted much of his research during the 1920s when he was frequently hospitalized or bedridden. He died at thirty-seven years of age.[165]

Cuba's Families Code is a World First

Like the Soviet Union, Cuba began its life as a socialist country besieged and beset. For the past sixty years, Washington has subjected this Caribbean island nation of eleven million people to the longest-lasting sanctions in foreign-policy history. These sanctions were meant to make ordinary Cubans suffer for choosing socialism. Washington's stated goal when the sanctions were implemented in 1962 was "to bring about hunger, desperation, and overthrow of government."[166] The sanctions, or more accurately, the blockade, have inflicted at least $147.8 billion in damages on the Cuban economy. It impacts every aspect of life on the island to this day.[167]

Even under such difficult circumstances, Cuba has come through with another first in human and disability rights. In September 2022, it passed the Families Code, what some call the most progressive family code in the world. The Families Code "modernizes, recognizes, and legalizes all manifestations of families in Cuba," with the detailed articulation of the rights of people with disabilities as one of the central features.[168]

Overwhelmingly approved by a national referendum, the Code guarantees the right of all people to form a family without discrimination. Called the Families Code because it recognizes many ways to build families, and it details the fullest inclusion of every family as a Cuban sees fit. The law defends equality, nondiscrimination, dignity, and respect for diversity.[169]

The code explicitly affirms the rights of people living "in a situation of disability" to a family life with dignity, to an autonomous and independent life, to choose a place of residence, and to a family life free of violence. This includes the right to form a family, to marry, to maternity and paternity, as well as the right to the means to do so.[170]

It affirms the right of people with disabilities to decide freely and responsibly the number of offspring, the way of having offspring, and the time that should elapse between one birth and another. The code also affirms their right to access information on sex education and family-planning issues appropriate for their age, in the case of children or adolescents, and that they should be offered the necessary means to enable them to exercise this right. Other provisions of the code broaden the family model to include the right to same-sex marriage, expand adoption rights, allow surrogacy births, add stronger protections against domestic violence, and explicitly expand the rights of children and seniors.[171]

A Social Model of Disabilities

The Families Code adopts a social or human rights model of disability. The code recognizes disability is not of the person as such but is due to barriers created by the society that impede or restrict them from full and effective participation in society. This definition is in line with the definition used in the United Nations International Convention on the Rights of Persons with Disabilities, which Cuba has signed and ratified, and whose measures it seeks to meet.

Associations of persons with disabilities took part in the design and monitoring of the policies that concerned them, and they had and continue to have a presence at all levels of the government.[172]

From the Family Code to the Civil Domain

The new code will govern the practice of family law in Cuba. It will guide the Civil Code in detailing rules that allow persons with disabilities to exercise their rights under equal conditions.[173] According to Leonardo Pérez, president of the Cuban Society of Civil and Family Law, this includes the rights of people with disabilities to family inclusion, self-determination, self-realization, and autonomy.

Also, to be further refined are measures to avoid discrimination against people with disabilities and the causes of situations of vulnerability. Further protections will ensure that those who support people with disabilities, when that support is needed, do not overstep their actions.[174]

Cuba Moves Forward while the US Retreats

In 1995, just five years after the Americans with Disabilities Act (ADA) was passed in the US, Cuba's first plan of action for people with disabilities was created. At that time, the US government, as previously described, did not implement the regulations needed to advance the ADA. Legislatures defunded areas of government that would implement the ADA. Elected officials turn away as employers and landlords blatantly violate the ADA. In roughly equal time frames since the ADA was passed, the US and Cuba have taken very different paths. Cuba has moved forward while the US has retreated.

While the ADA inspired the creation of the UN Convention on the Rights of People with Disabilities, the US Congress has not ratified it, as would be expected to meet the provisions outlined. Cuba's government has ratified the document and strives to meet all its measures.[175]

Cuba has moved forward, with the new Families Code being the latest refinement of disability rights. In 1990, the Cuban National Council to Support Persons with Disabilities was created to implement programs and policies. The rights of people with disabilities are included in the Social Security Act and the Labor Code, which ensures employment access without discrimination for all workers, including those in the non-state sector.

The 2019 Constitution of Cuba refines the 1976 Constitution to guarantee the right to equal salary for equal work, with explicit wording for people with disabilities. It charges the state, the family, and society with responsibility for the social inclusion of people with disabilities and for creating conditions for the free development of their personality. The 2022 Families Code replaces the Family Code of 1975 with further details of rights.[176]

Cuba Encourages Mass Participation, US Ignores or Limits It

In the US, we must protest in large numbers, often for many years, to force the government to pass progressive laws, and then we must fight to have them implemented. In Cuba, the government encourages the feedback of its population on important laws, incorporates the feedback, and then the whole population votes on the measure in question.

Six million Cubans attended thousands of workplace, neighborhood, and mass organization meetings to discuss the draft of the Families Code. Grassroots suggestions changed 49 percent of the code. The final version was overwhelmingly passed by 68 percent in a national referendum of five million voters.[177]

Biggest Obstacle to Cuba's Moving Forward is the US Blockade

But while its laws stand at the vanguard of policy on disability, Cuba is still struggling to implement accessibility and inclusion. The biggest obstacle to Cuba's development in all areas is the US blockade. Cuba has standards to create full accessibility in infrastructure.[178] The blockade, however, is so severe that it does not even permit Cuba to import building supplies it needs to replace the four thousand houses destroyed by Hurricane Ian that hit Cuba in September of 2022.

Cuban factories cannot get the materials to produce orthopedic assistance devices and must import them. While these devices are free to those who need them, there are often long waits for prostheses, such as artificial limbs, which must be imported.[179] The US blockade denies Cuba medications that are made with a US patent or have medical technology with US components. It even applies to importing food.

Housing, Jobs, and Education are Guaranteed

Good laws and their full implementation are not all that is needed for full equality and inclusion for people with disabilities. There is also the right to the means to support life—the right to a job, safe housing, nutritious food, education, and health and medical care. Cuba's constitution guarantees all of these rights as basic human rights. This makes a huge difference to people with disabilities. The US Constitution guarantees no such rights.

For example, people with disabilities are at high risk for homelessness in the US and homelessness is rising. In 2022, giant developers seeking profits have caused the biggest rent hikes in more than thirty years and, at the same time, are destroying affordable working-class housing. Workers must borrow hundreds of thousands of dollars to buy a house and pay the principal, plus many thousands of dollars more in interest to banks to keep their homes.[180] As a result, millions face imminent eviction on any given day because they cannot afford their rent or mortgage payment.[181]

In Cuba, there is no homelessness, and everyone has a place to live. Housing is not a commodity. It is a guaranteed human right. There are no real estate developers gobbling up apartments, as it is illegal to own more than one primary residence plus a vacation home. No one is held hostage to a housing loan at exorbitant interest rates. This Caribbean nation has one of the highest rates of home ownership in the world—85 percent. Of those who pay rent, it is never more than 10 percent of one's income.[182] In Cuba, education and job training are free at all levels.

Quality and Universal Health Care: A Pillar of the Cuban Revolution

Faced with a for-profit medical establishment that puts their needs last, the main concern of people with disabilities in the US is getting and keeping adequate health-care coverage.

In Cuba, high-quality and accessible health care for all citizens is one of the most important pillars of their revolution, with the expansion and improvement of health care among the government's highest priorities and largest budgetary allowances. All Cuban health care is regulated and financed by the government and is free of charge. Cuba spends a fraction of what the US spends on health care. Cuba's $6,928 per capita for health care is 73.68 percent lower than what is spent per person on health care in the United States.[183] Cuba can do this because there are no profit-driven HMOs to manage care, private hospitals to quadruple prices above costs, and no pharmaceutical monopolies to jack up drug prices hundreds of times above what they cost to make.

Compared to the US, Cuba's people, on the whole, are healthier. Cuban life expectancy is higher: in 2016, it was 80 compared to 78.69 in the US. Cuban infant mortality was lower in 2016, with 4.2 deaths per 1,000 live births as opposed to 5.6 in the US. Cuba has more doctors per person than the US, with 9 doctors per 1,000 inhabitants, the highest number in the world, while the US has 2.6 doctors[184] for every 1,000 inhabitants.[185]

With some medications and much medical technology denied by the embargo, Cuba focuses on preventing disease and disability. The embargo has compelled Cuba to make medications to meet its population's needs. This has led Cuba to develop some medications that are unique in the world—including vaccines for lung cancer and Meningococci B and C and Heberprot-P, the best medication for treating diabetic foot ulcers.

Cuban Health Care is Free and Community-Based

While US health care is costly with doctors often having practices far from their patients' homes, Cuban health care is free, with doctors and nurses living in the communities they serve. Every Cuban neigh-borhood—urban or rural—is assigned a family doctor, who is your neighbor, who is available twenty-four hours a day, and who has no time limit to patient sessions. These doctors are evaluated not by how many patients they see each day, but by how they improve the health of their communities.[186]

The doctor-nurse team keeps track of everyone and visits their homes at least once a year. During a home visit, the neighborhood medical team assesses health and general well-being. Do families have trouble buying food? Are homes in need of repair? Are social supports needed for individual members? Do people have jobs?[187] They do risk assessments and determine if follow-up home visits are needed or if, due to a disability, a patient needs to be seen in the home as a matter of course rather than in the office. Each person diagnosed with a "potential disability" is assigned a medical team.[188] Health-care services provide various rehabilitation services for adults with disabilities.[189]

Diabetes Treatment in Cuba

This approach pays off—not in profits for a few, but in health for the many. Take Cuba's approach to diabetes, for example. Due to its preventive measures at the primary-care level and its research in the field of diabetes, Cuba has achieved the best glycemic control. It has the lowest diabetes mortality rate in Latin America, according to the Pan-American Health Organization.[190]

The Cuban medical system is tailored first to prevent diabetes and then to identify people with diabetes before the disease advances and treat them immediately. There are special programs to assist diabetic women during pregnancy, children and teens with diabetes, and elders with chronic disease.

In Cuba, Insulin is Free

Cuba does not have access to continuous-monitoring blood-glucose meters or insulin-infusion pumps because they are made with US technology, and the embargo forbids their import. All Cuban patients, however, are guaranteed access to glucometers at no cost. While for-profit companies in the US price-gauge for insulin, this essential medication is free in Cuba.

What of diabetic amputations, which are on the rise in the US, especially in communities of color? Cuba's comprehensive diabetic care includes the drug Heberprot-P. The medication was developed by the Cuban Center for Genetic Engineering and Biotechnology and is free to those who need it. This is the only drug in the world capable of enhancing the healing of diabetic foot ulcers, a complex injury.[191] Its use has prevented lower limb amputations in 80 percent of Cubans with ulcers on their feet caused by diabetes.[192]

The US embargo, which prohibits the importation of Heberprot-P, denies Americans with diabetes from benefiting from this medication. It could prevent many of the 130,000 toe, foot, and leg amputations performed yearly.

Civil Society Pitches In

Cuba's medical/public health system doesn't just extend to every neighborhood. The Cuban population is organized into several mass organizations, with almost every Cuban belonging to at least one. These groups can help remove specific obstacles that might confront Cubans with disabilities.

There is the Federation of Cuban Women (FMC), whose goal is the full social integration of women and their development as leaders. The FMC also helps women with disabled children. It offers training for everyone on services created for the social integration of persons with disabilities.

Some 90 percent of Cuban workers are unionized and members of the Workers Central Union of Cuba, an organization which advocates for its members on and off the job.

Committees for the Defense of the Revolution are neighborhood groups organized by the block, by the building, or even by the floor in the case of large high-rise apartments. Its members check in on families, see if they have unmet needs, and help resolve issues such as social isolation and alienation.[193]

This chapter, which has provided examples of what can be done to address and advance the rights and needs of disabled people through the Russian and Cuban Revolutions, shows the superiority and greater humanity of socialism. Yet the potential of both revolutions to build societies where the needs of humanity are fully met has not been seen.

Both revolutions happened in countries that were economically underdeveloped. The capacity of the productive forces inherited from their capitalist exploiters was insufficient to fully address all the needs of the population. Additionally, they had to operate in a hostile capitalist-dominated world that imposed war and embargoes on them. Consequently, both countries had to allocate much-needed resources to national defense against invasion and counterrevolution by imperialism instead of meeting the needs of the people.

Imagine what a workers-run society could do with the technology, resources, and economic capacity of a country like the United States. That is the subject of the next and final chapter.

A SOCIALIST UNITED STATES AND THE LIBERATION OF PEOPLE WITH DISABILITIES

The significant advances in disability rights in the Soviet Union and Cuba, even under severe economic constraints, show socialism to be far superior to capitalism in meeting and advancing the social and economic needs of the people. Replacing capitalism with a socialist system lays the groundwork for expanding and securing full civil rights for all people, including people with disabilities.

Capitalists and their apologists spend much energy claiming capitalism can never be replaced by socialism, or that socialism might be okay for some other country but doesn't apply in the US. The truth is that socialism is not only realizable in the US, but it is also an urgent necessity. Income and wealth inequality is substantially higher in the US than in any other developed nation and is on the rise.[194] The greed of the capitalists knows no bounds. They must be stopped.

For example, the medical-industrial complex is making record profits by raising the cost of health care in the US.[195] What is the result? Medical bills are the leading cause of bankruptcy.[196] Millions of people are skipping their medication because they can't afford them.[197] As much as 25 percent of the population is delaying or not getting care because of skyrocketing costs.[198] Nearly forty-five thousand Americans die each year as a direct result of being unable to afford insurance.[199]

At the same time, 30 percent of all US households have rent or mortgage payments they cannot afford,[200] and people with disabilities have even higher rates of housing insecurity.[201] Most Americans are one crisis away from being homeless,[202] and the homelessness crisis is worsening.[203] Why? Giant real estate developers are demolishing working-class homes to build luxury housing which draws megaprofits. Investment firms and other speculators are buying up affordable homes and apartments, then deliberately keeping them off the market in order to raise rents. It's time to expropriate the expropriators and the government that represents them.

Unlike the USSR and Cuba, a socialist US would not begin with scarcity, but with abundance. The US already has the world's largest gross national product; it is second in the world in natural resources,[204] it is the world's top food exporter,[205] the first in high-tech manufacturing,[206] and the first in medical technology innovation.[207] With these resources, and the trillions stolen yearly in profits by the banks and the monopolies instead wrested from them into the hands of the workers whose toil made them possible, progressive change here could come very quickly.

A socialist government that is based on meeting the needs of the working class would recognize and take responsibility for guaranteeing and implementing basic human rights for all: the right to a full and productive life, to health and medical care, to be free of hunger, to have adequate and safe shelter, to a job at decent pay, and to dignity and respect, prioritizing previously marginalized communities.

At the same time, a socialist government would have no need for a predatory military that prowls the world to suppress liberation struggles and defend the extraction of superprofits by corporations at the people's expense. Dismantling the military-industrial complex and taking back the $1 trillion in tax dollars now going yearly to the Pentagon will liberate trillions of dollars to rectify the crimes committed by imperialist aggression abroad.

Guaranteeing all affordable and safe housing, free medical care, and an adequate income to meet all needs will go a long way to addressing the issues that people with disabilities have identified as top concerns.[208] But more would be needed. How might a socialist government make sure that disability rights are fully addressed?

Disability Rights and Accessibility Administration

One possibility is for the new government to create a Disability Rights and Accessibility Administration (DRAA). Run by people with disabilities, it would be charged with creating the conditions and building the programs for people living with disabilities to control their own lives, have self-realization and autonomy, be regarded with respect, and be valued and integrated into society. This government body would have the staff, resources, and the legal clout to accomplish these tasks.

The DRAA would make sure that people with disabilities are present and visible at all levels of government and employment. With people with disabilities fully in charge, it could do what this present capitalist government would not—develop a plan and protocols to implement all aspects of the ADA in employment, public accommodations, public services, transportation, housing, telecommunication, and community support.

Working-class and poor neighborhoods and the homeless population, which have the greatest percentages of people with disabilities, would get services first, and be prioritized in housing and jobs. Centers for Independent Living, which connect people with disabilities to information and resources, could be vastly expanded into every neighborhood. These centers could, at the same time, evaluate the unmet needs of people with disabilities in their areas and report to the DRAA on what needs to be improved.

Another priority would be ending the criminalization of disability, and the school-to-prison pipeline, which traps so many youth with disabilities, and liberating the hundreds of thousands of people with mostly mental health disabilities from prisons and jails and into appropriate housing and treatment.

Health Care

A socialist government would abolish the medical-industrial complex and make it a crime to profit from health care or medications, or to shun some patients in favor of others. There will be no such thing as privately owned intellectual property. Formulas for medications will be made available to the world.

All health care, medication, assistive devices such as wheelchairs, hearing aids, artificial limbs, and other forms of medical care and equipment would be free. The US is the source of some of the most cutting-edge, high-tech medicine and medical inventions. Such advanced care would be free and available to all.

Doctors, no longer supervised by accountants and pressured to limit visits to fifteen minutes, will get the respect and time they need to care for patients. They would be held responsible and monitored for the quality of care they deliver and how well they maintain and improve the health of their patients, especially those with disabilities—not for how many they see in a day.

Clinics and community mental health services could be quickly moved to neighborhoods, rural and urban. Each neighborhood center would be fitted with an exam table that can be dialed to different heights and a scale that could accommodate wheelchairs. If there is a shortage initially, wheelchair users would have access to free car service access to a medical facility that has the environment and equipment to properly provide care.

The neighborhood medical team would make home visits. Community members would also have twenty-four-hour access to community doctors via phone, email, or videoconference as they will be provided with free smartphones and Wi-Fi. Accessible shuttle buses or accessible taxis will be available to people with disabilities who may need them booked in advance and punctual in going and returning from major hospitals for advanced diagnostic testing and treatments.

Housing

Working with architects and engineers, the DRAA would develop and implement a plan for eliminating architectural barriers in housing, school, transportation, workplaces, public spaces, and more. Workplaces and new housing would be codesigned to meet the needs of as many as possible and would be beautiful at the same time.

Following the Cuban example, no one will be allowed to have more than one home and a vacation home, rent will not be more than 10 percent of one's income, and people will be able to buy their homes at highly affordable prices. Utilities will be affordable, if not free. Heat and electricity will be free.

Giant real estate developers will be abolished and their properties confiscated. Luxury and high-rent apartments, many of which are unoccupied,[209] will be commandeered for those whose housing is the most unsafe. With less than 5 percent of housing nationwide accessible for people with moderate mobility difficulties,[210] and less than 1 percent for wheelchair users,[211] people with disabilities who have functional needs that are not met where they live will be among those prioritized for accessible housing.

There will be no parasitic landlords to make massive profits off rentals or to buy up large quantities of homes or apartments and hold them off the market in order to raise prices. Tens of thousands of empty and warehoused housing units will be confiscated by the government and renovated for working-class families, with priority given to people with disabilities to live in buildings close to public transportation, buildings close to places of employment, ground-floor apartments, and elevator buildings and units that can most easily be accommodated for accessibility. If people become disabled and choose to remain in their current homes, they would have the right to have them renovated—doorways, bathrooms, kitchens, etc., as needed, for free or at very low costs.

Priority will be given to refurbishing and maintaining the country's public housing units and the elevators in these buildings, as large numbers of people with disabilities live in these homes.

Jobs

Lower wage-scales for people with disabilities or anyone else will be abolished. And all workers, including people with disabilities and their caregivers, will be guaranteed enough money to meet their needs and to flourish. There will be plenty of jobs, as there will be so much to do in building the new society. With only 19.1 percent of people with disabilities currently working, they will be among those prioritized for jobs and training. The opportunity for remote work, modified hours, and flexible schedules will be made available immediately to people with disabilities on any job where that is possible. Discrimination in hiring on the job will be against the law and the law will be enforced.

Transportation

There will be a vast expansion of accessible public transportation of all kinds. Those who would be homebound without owning a car will have vehicles, refitted as needed, for a nominal cost, and eventually for free.

The need for wheelchair-fitted or kneel buses, elevators, ramps, adequate restrooms and accessible trains on subways, and beacons in subways that let people with low vision navigate would be assessed by local offices. With the billions in wealth and resources that were stolen by the displaced capitalists reclaimed by the socialist government on behalf of the workers who produced that wealth, there will be more than enough resources to address the needs of disabled and able-bodied people.

Just as there is GPS to guide travelers and apps to navigate large public transit systems, apps can be created to find accessible travel routes. These apps could also collect data on trip length for accessible rides to various destinations and find out which routes are most used by people in need of accommodation to be prioritized for better access.

Breaking Down Barriers and Building Bridges

With no exploiter defining others as "less than" to justify exploitation, under socialism, the material basis for ableism, sexism, racism, chauvinism, or any form of belittlement and oppression will disappear. Education, however, will still be needed to counter the racism, sexism, homophobia, and stigmatization of disability inherited from capitalism. Educating all people about disability civil rights will create empathy and motivate people to understand that it's everyone's responsibility to remove those barriers so we can all take part in society equally.

The DRAA would identify ways to create a positive culture around disabilities. The presence of people with disabilities will be made more visible in all areas of life, including entertainment, with the goal of making disabled representation commonplace. The DRAA will control the narrative on how this is done to ensure it avoids ableist assumptions.

This would be just the beginning of breaking down barriers and building bridges instead. Socialism will create the foundation for the full development of each person's potential, for defining each person by their gifts, and for cherishing them for their contribution to the community.

ENDNOTES

Chapter One: The Social Construction of 'Disability' in the US

1   "Disability Impacts ALL of US," Centers for Disease Control and Prevention, accessed November 23, 2022, https://www.cdc.gov/ncbddd/disabilityandhealth/pdf/330379-A-IG_DisabilityImpactsAllofUsInfographic_v3-5-15-P.pdf.

2   "Mental Illness," National Institute of Mental Health, updated January 2022, https://www.nimh.nih.gov/health/statistics/mental-illness#.

3   Ibid.

4   James Gorman, "Ancient Bones That Tell a Story of Compassion," *New York Times*, December 12, 2021, https://www.nytimes.com/2012/12/18/science/ancient-bones-that-tell-a-story-of-compassion.html/.

5   Joyce Chediac, "Disability Rights in the Age of Austerity," *Workers World*, July 31, 2014, https://www.workers.org/2014/07/15489/.

6   "The Lives of Medieval Peasants," Saylor Foundation, accessed December 26, 2022, https://resources.saylor.org/wwwresources/archived/site/wp-content/uploads/2012/10/HIST201-1.1.4-MedievalPeasants-FINAL1.pdf/

7   Journal of Christopher Columbus, *The American Yawp Reader*, accessed November 23, 2022, https://www.americanyawp.com/reader/the-new-world/journal-of-christopher-columbus/.

8   Minerva Rivas Velarde, "Indigenous Perspectives of Disability," *Disability Studies Quarterly* 38 , no. 4 (Fall 2018), https://dsq-sds.org/article/view/6114/5134/.

9   Kim E. Nielsen, *Disability History of the United States* (United States: Beacon Press, 2012), 20.

10 Nielsen, *Disability History*, 101.

11 Douglas Baynton, "Disability and the Justification of Inequality in American History," Disability History Museum, accessed December 26, 2022, http://www.disabilitymuseum.org/dhm/edu/essay.html?id=70/.

12 Nielsen, *Disability History*, 42.

13 Susan M.Schweik, *The Ugly Laws: Disability in Public* (United Kingdom: NYU Press, 2010), 291.

14   Nielsen, *Disability History*, 80.

15   "The Philippine-American War, 1899–1902," Office of the Historian, US Department of State, accessed December 26, 2022, https://history.state.gov/milestones/1899-1913/war/.

16   "'The White Man's Burden': Kipling's Hymn to U.S. Imperialism," History Matters, quoted in Rudyard Kipling, "The White Man's Burden: The United States & The Philippine Islands, 1899." *Rudyard Kipling's Verse: Definitive Edition* (Garden City, New York: Doubleday, 1929), accessed December 26, 2022, https://historymatters.gmu.edu/d/5478/.

17   Alexandra Minna Stern, "That Time the United States Sterilized 60,000 of its Citizens," *Huffington Post*, January 7, 2016, https://www.huffpost.com/entry/sterilization-united-states_n_568f35f2e4b0c8beacf68713/.

18   "1907 Indiana Eugenics Law," Indiana Historical Bureau, accessed November 23, 2022, https://www.in.gov/history/state-historical-markers/find-a-marker/1907-indiana-eugenics-law/.

19   Nielsen, *Disability History*, 69.

20   Manon S. Parry, "Dorothea Dix (1802–1887)," *American Journal of Public Health* 96, no. 4 (2006): 624–625, accessed November 23, 2022, https://doi.org/10.2105/AJPH.2005.079152/.

21   Curtis Flory, MBA and Rose Marie Friedrich, RN, MA, "Half a Million Mental Patients Liberated from Institutions to Community Settings Without Provision for Long-Term Care," MentalIllnesspolicy.org, accessed November 23, 2022, https://mentalillnesspolicy.org/imd/deinstitutionalization-flory.html/.

22   Dean H. Aufderheide and Patrick H. Brown, "Crisis in Corrections: The Mentally Ill in America's Prison," *Corrections Today* 67, no 1 (2005): 30–33, accessed November 23, 2022, https://www.ojp.gov/ncjrs/virtual-library/abstracts/crisis-corrections-mentally-ill-americas-prison.

23   Zeb Larson, "America's Long-Suffering Mental Health System," Origins: Current Events in Historical Perspective, Ohio State University, April 2018, https://origins.osu.edu/article/americas-long-suffering-mental-health-system/.

24   Ari Melber and Marti Hause, "Half Of People Killed By Police Have A Disability: Report," NBC News, March 14, 2016, https://namiillinois.org/half-people-killed-police-disability-report/.

25   Nielsen, *Disability History*, 162

26   "An estimated 100,000 people with disabilities are paid less than $7.25 an hour," Office of Senator Bob Casey of Pennsylvania, November 18, 2021, https://www.casey.senate.gov/news/releases/casey-daines-introduce-bipartisan-bill-to-phase-out-subminimum-wage-increase-competitive-Integrated-employment-for-people-with-disabilities.

Chapter Two: Every Advance Requires a Fight

27   "About Us," National Association of the Deaf, accessed November 23, 2022, https://www.nad.org/about-us/.

28   Kaleigh O'Keefe, "Helen Keller a socialist? Who knew!," *Liberation News*, July 25, 2021, https://www.liberationnews.org/helen-keller-a-socialist-who-knew/.

29 Keller to Robert La Follette, July 27, 1924, Helen Keller Archive, https://www.afb.org/ HelenKellerArchive?a=d&d=A-HK01-03-B066-F12-003.1.1&srpos=1/.

30 "The work of the American Federation of the Physically Handicapped, Inc.," American Federation of the Physically Handicapped, Inc., undated, https://library.uta.edu/ txdisabilityhistory/doc/20001886.

31 Ibid.

32 Mike Ervin, "Mike Ervin: Protesting Jerry Lewis' charity mentality," *Lompoc Record*, August 27, 2017, https://lompocrecord.com/opinion/columnists/mike-ervin-protesting-jerry-lewis-charity-mentality/article_2022e44f-7523-5c4a-9ea8-fd4638280124.html/.

33 Jon Wiener, "The End of the Jerry Lewis Telethon—It's About Time," *The Nation*, September 2, 2011, https://www.thenation.com/article/archive/end-jerry-lewis-telethon-its-about-time/.

34 Travis M. Andrews, "Jerry Lewis telethons raised billions for muscular dystrophy. Many cheered when he went off the air," *Washington Post*, August 21, 2017, https://www.washingtonpost.com/news/morning-mix/wp/2017/08/21/jerry-lewis-telethons-raised-billions-for-muscular-dystrophy-many-cheered-when-he-went-off-the-air/; Mike Ervin, "The Jerry Lewis Telethon Could Have Had a Happy Ending," *The Progressive Magazine*, August 23, 2017, https://progressive.org/latest/jerry-lewis-telethon-could-have-had-a-happy-ending-170823/.

35 Emily Wolinsky, "Dear Kevin Hart, The MDA is Heartless," Disability Visibility Project, October 12, 2020, https://disabilityvisibilityproject.com/2020/10/12/ dear-kevin-hart-the-mda-is-heartless/.

36 *Crip Camp*. Directed by Nicole Newnham and Jim LeBrecht, Higher Ground and Rusted Spoke Productions, 2020. YouTube, https://www.youtube.com/ watch?v=OFS8SpwioZ4.

37 "Crip Camp Curriculum," Crip Camp, accessed November 24, 2022, https://cripcamp. com/education-materials/.

38 "The Black Panthers and Disability History," *Independence Now*, February 12, 2021, https://www.innow.org/2021/02/12/black-panthers/.

39 "Brad Lomax—Uniting the Civil Rights and Disability Rights Communities," The Center for Learner Equity, February 12, 2021, https://www.centerforlearnerequity.org/ news/brad-lomax-uniting-the-civil-rights-and-disability-rights-communities/.

40 Nicole Newnham and Jim LeBrecht, *Crip Camp.*

41 "ADAPT's Community for ALL Platform," ADAPT, accessed November 24, 2022, https://adapt.org/adapts-community-for-all-platform/.

42 Ibid.

43 ADAPT, https://www.adapt.org/.

44 King Jordan, "King Jordan's account of the DPN protest," Gallaudet University, accessed November 24, 2022, https://gallaudet.edu/museum/history/the-deaf-president-now-dpn-protest/i-king-jordans-account-of-the-dpn-protest/.

45 "An Overview of the Americans With Disabilities Act," National Network: Information, Guidance, and Training on the Americans with Disabilities Act, accessed November 24, 2022, https://adata.org/factsheet/ADA-overview/.

46   https://twitter.com/KimKrawiec/status/1477016163376840706, Alice Wong, "Those inequities carried through to the pandemic. Dialysis patients who were Black or L..." https://twitter.com/SFdirewolf/status/1503322804678115333?ref_src=twsrc%5Etfw

47   Alice Wong, "I'm disabled and need a ventilator to live. Am I expendable during this pandemic?," *Vox*, April 4, 2020, https://www.vox.com/first-person/2020/4/4/21204261/coronavirus-covid-19-disabled-people-disabilities-triage/.

48   Alice Wong, "Disabled Activist Speaks Out Against Ableism During Pandemic," interview by Rachel Scheier, *Truthout*, February 5, 2022, https://truthout.org/articles/disabled-activist-speaks-out-against-ableism-during-pandemic/.

49   Carrie Ann Lucas, "The disability community lost one of its fiercest advocates on 2/24/19," Facebook, February 24, 2019, https://www.facebook.com/CarrieAnnLucasPersonal/posts/10217145330961609/.

50   Robyn Powell, "Carrie Ann Lucas, Disability Rights Activist and Attorney, Dies Following Denial From Insurance Company," *Rewire News Group*, February 25, 2019, https://rewirenewsgroup.com/article/2019/02/25/carrie-ann-lucas-disability-rights-activist-and-attorney-dies-following-denial-from-insurance-company/.

51   "About Us," Hand in Hand, accessed November 24, 2022, https://domesticemployers.org/about/.

52   Blithe Riley, "Hand in Hand grieves the loss of Engracia Figueroa," Hand in Hand, accessed November 24, 2022, https://domesticemployers.org/hand-in-hand-grieves-the-loss-of-engracia-figueroa/.

53   Laken Brooks, "Disability Advocate Engracia Figueroa Died After an Airline Damaged Her Wheelchair," *Forbes*, November 8, 2021, https://www.forbes.com/sites/lakenbrooks/2021/11/08/disability-advocate-engracia-figueroa-died-after-an-airline-damaged-her-wheelchair/.

54   Gabriela Miranda, "Disability Rights Activist, Who Shared Her Story about Airline Damaging Her Wheelchair, Dies," *USA Today*, November 5, 2021, https://www.usatoday.com/story/travel/airline-news/2021/11/05/activist-who-highlighted-airline-damage-wheelchairs-dies/6297761001/.

55   "Air Travel Consumer Report," Office of Aviation Consumer Protection, February 2022, https://www.transportation.gov/sites/dot.gov/files/2022-02/February%20 2022%20ATCR.pdf.

56   Amanda Morris, "Embarrassing, Uncomfortable and Risky: What Flying is Like for Passengers Who Use Wheelchairs," *New York Times*, August 8, 2022, https://www.nytimes.com/2022/08/08/travel/air-travel-wheelchair.html/.

57   Miranda, "Disability Rights Activist."

58   Ibid.

Chapter Three: Building Solidarity between Care Workers and Clients

59   Liz Donovan and Muriel Alarcón, "Long Hours, Low Pay, Loneliness and a Booming Industry," *New York Times*, September 25, 2021 and updated November 1, 2021, https://www.nytimes.com/2021/09/25/business/home-health-aides-industry.html/.

60   "Home Health Aide Job Description: Top Duties and Qualifications," Indeed.com, accessed November 24, 2022, https://www.indeed.com/hire/job-description/home-health-aide/.

61 Theresa A. Allison, MD, PhD; Anna Oh, PhD, MPH, RN; and Krista L. Harrison, PhD; "Extreme Vulnerability of Home Care Workers During the COVID-19 Pandemic—A Call to Action," JAMA Network, August 4, 2020, https://jamanetwork.com/journals/jamainternalmedicine/fullarticle/2769095/.

62 "Declaration of Emergency: Home and Community-Based Services Waivers Community Choices Waiver Direct Support/Service Worker Wages and Bonus Payments (LAC 50: XXI. Chapter 95)," Department of Health Bureau of Health Services Financing and Office of Aging and Adult Services, August 1, 2022, https://doa.la.gov/media/m5ijyqnn/2301emr006.pdf.

63 Elizabeth Hinton and Lina Stolyar, "10 Things to Know About Medicaid Managed Care," Kaiser Family Foundation, February 23, 2022, https://www.kff.org/medicaid/issue-brief/10-things-to-know-about-medicaid-managed-care/.

64 Larry DeWitt, "The Decision to Exclude Agricultural and Domestic Workers from the 1935 Social Security Act," *Social Security Bulletin* 70 no. 4 (2010): 49, https://www.ssa.gov/policy/docs/ssb/v70n4/v70n4p49.html/.

65 Robin D.G. Kelley, *Hammer and Hoe: Alabama Communists During the Great Depression* (Chapel Hill and London: University of North Carolina Press, 1990), 4.

66 Ibid, 21.

67 "FACT SHEET: The American Jobs Plan," The White House, March 31, 2021, https://www.whitehouse.gov/briefing-room/statements-releases/2021/03/31/fact-sheet-the-american-jobs-plan/.

68 Vanessa Barrington, "Biden Administration Signals Continued Commitment to Home Care After Build Back Better Stall," Justice In Aging, February 18, 2022, https://justiceinaging.org/biden-administration-signals-continued-commitment-to-home-care-after-build-back-better-stall/.

69 Cummie Davis, "VOICES: Health Care Workers Urge NC Lawmakers to Pass $15 Minimum Wage," *Facing South*, April 26, 2021, https://www.facingsouth.org/2021/04/voices-health-care-workers-urge-nc-lawmakers-pass-15-minimum-wage/.

70 Ibid.

71 Ibid.

72 Rebekah Barber, "Low-wage Care Workers Rally for the American Jobs Plan," *Facing South*, June 16, 2021, https://www.facingsouth.org/2021/06/low-wage-care-workers-rally-american-jobs-plan/.

73 "Homecare," SEIU 1199, accessed November 24, 2022, https://www.1199seiu.org/homecare/.

74 John Daly, personal communication with Michael Luciano, April 14, 2022.

75 Donovan and Alarcón, "Long Hours, Low Pay."

76 "Boot the Braids! . . . Student-led Wendy's campaign set to hit the road running this coming school year!," Coalition of Immokalee Workers, August 26, 2014, https://ciw-online.org/blog/2014/08/encuentro

77 "Fair Food Program: The Power of Prevention," Coalition of Immokalee Workers, accessed November 24, 2022, https://fairfoodprogram.org/.

Chapter Four: Killer and Disabler of Millions

78   Masao Tomonaga, "The Atomic Bombings of Hiroshima and Nagasaki: A Summary of the Human Consequences, 1945-2018, and Lessons for Homosapiens to End the Nuclear Weapon Age," *Journal for Peace and Nuclear Disarmament*, 2 no. 2 (2019): 491-517, https://www.tandfonline.com/doi/full/10.1080/25751654.2019.1681226/.

79   Xuan Dung Phan, "Greater US efforts in Supporting Vietnamese Agent Orange Victims," East Asia Forum Economics, Politics and Public Policy in East Asia and the Pacific, January 24 2020, https://www.eastasiaforum.org/2020/01/24/greater-us-efforts-in-supporting-vietnamese-agent-orange-victims/.

80   Emma Stone, "Toxic legacy of Agent Orange lives on in Vietnam," *Chemistry World*, June 2, 2016, https://www.chemistryworld.com/news/toxic-legacy-of-agent-orange-lives-on-in-vietnam/1010367.article/.

81   George Black, "The Victims of Agent Orange the U.S. Has Never Acknowledged," *New York Times*, March 16, 2021, https://www.nytimes.com/2021/03/16/magazine/laos-agent-orange-vietnam-war.html/.

82   Charles Dunst, "The U.S.'s Toxic Agent Orange Legacy," *The Atlantic*, July 20, 2019, https://www.theatlantic.com/international/archive/2019/07/agent-orange-cambodia-laos-vietnam/591412/.

83   George Black, "The Victims of Agent Orange the U.S. Has Never Acknowledged," *New York Times*, March 16, 2021, https://www.nytimes.com/2021/03/16/magazine/laos-agent-orange-vietnam-war.html/.

84   Haley Foster, "Agent Orange: It's Affecting Veterans and Their Kids," North Dakota Depart of Veterans Affairs, March 19, 2015, https://www.veterans.nd.gov/news/agent-orange-its-affecting-veterans-and-their-kids/.

85   "Agent Orange," Veterans for Peace, accessed November 25, 2022, https://www.veteransforpeace.org/our-work/vfp-national-projects/agent-orange/.

86   Martha Graybow, "Court upholds dismissal of 'agent orange' suit," *Reuters*, February 25, 2008, https://www.reuters.com/article/us-agentorange-lawsuit/court-upholds-dismissal-of-agent-orange-suit-idUSN2257383520080225/.

87   Ibid.

88   "Vietnam," MAG, accessed November 25, 2022, https://www.maginternational.org/what-we-do/where-we-work/vietnam/.

89   "Explosive Remnants of War: Landmines, Clusterbombs, etc.," Veterans for Peace, Philadelphia, PA

90   Ibid.

91   "US broke its own rules firing depleted uranium in Iraq," PAX, accessed November 25, 2022, https://paxforpeace.nl/news/overview/us-broke-its-own-rules-firing-depleted-uranium-in-iraq/.

92   Samuel Oakford, "Depleted Uranium in Syria," *Foreign Policy*, February 14, 2017, https://foreignpolicy.com/2017/02/14/the-united-states-used-depleted-uranium-in-syria/.

93   Kali Rubaii, "Birth Defects and the Toxic Legacy of War in Iraq," Middle East Research and Information Project, September 22, 2020, https://merip.org/2020/09/birth-defects-and-the-toxic-legacy-of-war-in-iraq/.

94 "Media," Hunterseven Foundation, accessed November 25, 2022, https://hunterseven. org/about-us/media/.

95 Kelsey D. Atherton, "U.S. Forces Are Leaving a Toxic Environmental Legacy in Afghanistan, *Scientific American*, August 30, 2021, https://www.scientificamerican. com/article/u-s-forces-are-leaving-a-toxic-environmental-legacy-in-afghanistan/.

96 Elizabeth Roberts-Pedersen, "From Shell Shock to PTSD: Proof of War's Traumatic History," *The Conversation*, April 14, 2015, https://theconversation.com/ from-shell-shock-to-ptsd-proof-of-wars-traumatic-history-37858/.

97 "Post Traumatic Stress: Psychological Problems & Vietnam Vets,"Vietnam Veterans Against the War, accessed November 25, 2022, http://www.vvaw.org/veteran/ article/?id=2419/.

98 Roberts-Pedersen, "From Shell Shock to PTSD: Proof of War's Traumatic History."

99 Post-traumatic Stress Disorder (PTSD) Statistics: 2024 Update," Center for Advancing Health, accessed March16, 2024, https://cfah.org/ptsd-statistics/.

100 Ryan Devereaux and Murtaza Hussain, "Daniel Hale Sentenced to 45 Months in Prison for Drone Leak," *The Intercept*, July 27, 2021, https://theintercept.com/2021/07/27/ daniel-hale-drone-leak-sentencing/.

101 In USA v. Daniel Hale (EXHIBIT A Case 1:19-cr-00059-LO), Daniel Hale's Letter to the Court Ahead of Sentencing, https://www.documentcloud.org/documents/21015287- halelettertocourt?responsive=1&title=1ptsd quote from veteran/.

102 "TBI Among Service Members and Veterans," Centers for Disease Control and Prevention, accessed November 25, 2022, https://www.cdc.gov/traumaticbraininjury/ military/index.html/.

103 Scott Janssen, "I Work With Dying Veterans. Here's Why I Don't Automatically Thank Them for Their Service," *Huffington Post*, January 22, 2022, https://www.huffpost. com/entry/war-veterans-thank-you-service_n_61df1b97e4b0ee023e692528/.

104 Richard Sisk, "Alarming VA Report Totals Decade of Veteran Suicides," Military.com, September 23, 2019, https://www.military.com/daily-news/2019/09/23/alarming-va- report-totals-decade-veteran-suicides.html/.

105 Amy Morin, LCSW, "Homeless Veterans Living With PTSD," Verywellmind, March 4, 2020, https://www.verywellmind.com/homeless-veterans-living-with-ptsd-4164824/.

106 "Veteran Homelessness Facts," Green Doors, accessed November 25, 2022, https:// greendoors.org/facts/veteran-homelessness.php/.

107 John Lindsay-Poland and Nick Morgan, "Overseas Military Bases and Environment," Institute for Policy Studies, June 1, 1998, https://ips-dc.org/ overseas_military_bases_and_environment/.

108 Katherine T. McCaffrey, "Fish, Wildlife, and Bombs: The struggle to Clean Up Vieques," North American Congress on Latin America, September 1, 2009, https:// nacla.org/article/fish-wildlife-and-bombs-struggle-clean-vieques/.

109 Christina Jedra, "How The Red Hill Fuel System Has Threatened Oahu's Drinking Water For Decades," *Honolulu Civil Beat*, December 12, 2021, https://www.civilbeat. org/2021/12/how-the-red-hill-fuel-system-has-threatened-oahus-drinking-water-for- decades/.

110 Sophia McCullough, "Confused about the timeline for the Red Hill fuel storage facility and contaminated water? Read this," *Hawai'i Public Radio*, March 1, 2022, https://www.hawaiipublicradio.org/local-news/2021-12-21/confused-about-the-timeline-for-the-red-hill-fuel-storage-facility-and-contaminated-water-read-this/.

111 Alex Horton and Karoun Demirjian, "Military Families Say They Were Ill Months Before Jet-fuel Leak Brought Scrutiny to Pearl Harbor's Tap Water, *Washington Post*, December 22, 2021, https://www.washingtonpost.com/national-security/2021/12/21/pearl-harbor-water-contamination/.

112 Corinne Roels, Briana Smith and Adrienne St. Clair, "Military Bases' Contamination Will Affect Water for Generations," The Center for Public Integrity, August 18, 2017, https://publicintegrity.org/environment/military-bases-contamination-will-affect-water-for-generations/.

113 Jon Mitchell, "US Military Bases Are Poisoning Okinawa," *The Diplomat*, October 12, 2020, https://thediplomat.com/2020/10/us-military-bases-are-poisoning-okinawa/.

114 Roels, Smith and St. Clair, *Military Bases' Contamination Will Affect Water for Generations*.

115 Lindsay-Poland and Morgan, *Overseas Military Bases and Environment*.

Chapter Five: The Status of Rights for People with Disabilities

116 Susan K. Donius, "From the Archives: A Landmark Moment for Americans with Disabilities," Obama White House archives, July 26, 20212, https://obamawhitehouse.archives.gov/blog/2012/07/26/archives-landmark-moment-americans-disabilities/.

117 Justin Dart, "ADA: Landmark Declaration of Equality," *Work Life: A Publication on Employment and Persons with Disabilities*, Volume 3, Issues 1-4, Spring 1990, https://books.google.com/books?id=tfc68gASi5oC&pg=RA2-PA1&lpg=RA2-PA1&dq=#v=onepage&q&f=false/.

118 "Convention on the Rights of Persons with Disabilities, United Nations, accessed December 6, 2022, https://www.un.org/development/desa/disabilities/convention-on-the-rights-of-persons-with-disabilities/convention-on-the-rights-of-persons-with-disabilities-2.html/.

119 Abigail Abrams, "Years After a Landmark Disability Law, the Fight for Access and Equality Continues," *Time*, July 23, 2020, https://time.com/5870468/americans-with-disabilities-act-coronavirus/.

120 Ryan Golden, "Why Do Pay Gaps Persist for US Workers with Disabilities?" *HR Dive*, July 16, 2020, https://www.hrdive.com/news/why-do-pay-gaps-persist-for-us-workers-with-disabilities/581533/.

121 Jaboa Lake, Valerie Novack, and Mia Ives-Rublee, "Recognizing and Addressing Housing Insecurity for Disabled Renters," Center for American Progress, May 27, 2021, https://www.americanprogress.org/article/recognizing-addressing-housing-insecurity-disabled-renters/.

122 Colleen Heflin, Claire Altman, and Laura Rodriguez, "Having a Disability Increases The Likelihood of Food Insecurity Despite Federal Programs to Prevent This Hardship," Lerner Center for Public Health Promotion and Population Health, Population Health Research Brief Series, Syracuse University, September 2019, https://www.maxwell.syr.edu/research/lerner-center/population-health-research-brief-series/article/having-

a-disability-increases-the-likelihood-of-food-insecurity-despite-federal-programs-to-prevent-this-hardship?redirect

123 Abrams, "Years After a Landmark Disability Law."

124 Persons with a Disability: Labor Force Characteristics — 2023, Bureau of Labor Statistics, US Department of Labor, February 22, 2024, https://www.bls.gov/news.release/pdf/disabl.pdf/.

125 Michelle Maroto and David Pettinicchio, "The Limitations of Disability Antidiscrimination Legislation: Policymaking and the Economic Well-being of People with Disabilities," *Law & Policy* 36, no. 4 (October 2014), https://www.davidpettinicchio.com/uploads/1/5/4/8/15484818/thelimitations_of_antidiscrimination_legislation_lapol.pdf/.

126 Ibid.

127 Ibid.

128 Lake, Novack, and Ives-Rublee, "Recognizing and Addressing Housing Insecurity for Disabled Renters."

129 Fair Housing and Equal Opportunity, US Housing and Urban Development, ,https://www.hud.gov/program_offices/fair_housing_equal_opp/disability_main/.

130 Luke Bo'sher, Sewin Chan, Ingrid Gould Ellen, Brian Karfunkel, and Hsi-Ling Liao, "Accessibility of America's Housing Stock: Analysis of the 2011 American Housing Survey (AHS)", Office of Policy Development and Research, US Housing and Urban Development, May 26, 2015, https://www.huduser.gov/portal/publications/mdrt/accessibility-america-housingStock.html?q=publications%2Fmdrt%2Faccessibility-america-housingStock.html/.

131 Andrew Aurand, Ph.D., MSW; Dan Emmanuel, MSW; Daniel Threet, Ph.D.; Ikra Rafi, and Diane Yentel, "The Gap: A Shortage of Affordable Homes," National Low Income Housing Coalition, March 2021, https://reports.nlihc.org/sites/default/files/gap/Gap-Report_2021.pdf/.

132 Mark Battersby, "New York is Now World's Most Wealthy City Says Henley Global Citizens Report 2022," *Investment International*, September 14, 2022, https://investment-international.com/News/new-york-is-now-worlds-most-wealthy-city-says-henley-global-citizens-report-2022/.

133 "List of Cities by Number of Billionaires," *Wikipedia*, accessed March 17, 2024, https://en.wikipedia.org/wiki/List_of_cities_by_number_of_billionaires/.

134 Nanette Goodman, Michael Morris, and Kelvin Boston, "Financial Inequality: Disability, Race and Poverty in America," National Disability Institute, 2016, http://www.advancingstates.org/sites/nasuad/files/Disability-Race-Poverty-in-America.pdf/.

135 Shawn Fremstad, "Half in Ten: Why Taking Disability into Account is Essential to Reducing Income Poverty and Expanding Economic Inclusion," Center for Economic and Policy Research, September 2009, https://www.cepr.net/documents/publications/poverty-disability-2009-09.pdf/.

136 Erin Vinoski Thomas, PhD, CHES; and Chloe Vercruysse, MBA, " Homelessness Among Individuals with Disabilities: Influential Factors and Scalable Solutions," *JPHMP Direct*, July 24, 2019, https://jphmpdirect.com/2019/07/24/homelessness-among-individuals-with-disabilities/.

137 Meghan Henry, Tanya de Sousa, Caroline Roddey, Swati Gayen, and Thomas Joe Bednar, "The 2020 Annual Homeless Assessment Report (AHAR) to Congress", US Department of Housing and Urban Development, https://www.huduser.gov/portal/sites/default/files/pdf/2020-AHAR-Part-1.pdf/.

138 "Demographics Related to Women with Disabilities," Center for Research on Women with Disabilities, Baylor College of Medicine, accessed March 18, 2024, https://www.bcm.edu/research/research-centers/center-for-research-on-women-with-disabilities/demographics/.

139 Goodman, Morris, and Boston, "Financial Inequality: Disability, Race and Poverty in America."

140 Sandy Murillo, "Top Three Pressing Issues for Americans with Disabilities," *The Chicago Lighthouse*, accessed December 6, 2022, https://chicagolighthouse.org/sandys-view/top-three-pressing-issues-for-americans-with-disabilities/.

141 "Status of State Medicaid Expansion Decisions: Interactive Map," Kaiser Family Foundation, November 9, 2022, https://www.kff.org/medicaid/issue-brief/status-of-state-medicaid-expansion-decisions-interactive-map/.

142 Matthew Buettgens and Urmi Ramchandani, "Research Report: 3.7 Million People Would Gain Health Coverage in 2023 If the Remaining 12 States Were to Expand Medicaid Eligibility," Urban Institute, August 3, 2022, https://www.urban.org/research/publication/3-7-million-people-would-gain-health-coverage-2023-if-remaining-12-states-were/.

143 Neil Bennett, Jonathan Eggleston, Laryssa Mykyta and Briana Sullivan, "19% of U.S. Households Could Not Afford to Pay for Medical Care Right Away," Census.gov, April 07, 2021, https://www.census.gov/library/stories/2021/04/who-had-medical-debt-in-united-states.html/.

144 Kimberly Amadeo, "Medical Bankruptcy and the Economy: Do Medical Bills Really Devastate America's Families?" the balance, updated on January 20, 2022, https://www.thebalancemoney.com/medical-bankruptcy-statistics-4154729/.

145 Bennett, Eggleston, Mykyta and Sullivan, "Nineteen Percent of U.S. Households Could not Afford to Pay for Medical Care Right Away."

146 Rachel Berger, "Hospitals Focusing on Maximizing Profits are Cutting Labor and Delivery Units, Endangering Pregnant Patients and Entire Communities," National Nurses United, April-May-June 2022,https://www.nationalnursesunited.org/article/labor-pains/.

147 "New Study — Hospitals Hike Charges by Up to 18 Times Cost," National Nurses United, November 16, 2020, https://www.nationalnursesunited.org/press/new-study-hospitals-hike-charges-18-times-cost/.

148 Arielle Dreher, "Rural Hospitals Face Funding Cliff with $600 Million on the Line," Axios, September 21, 2022, https://www.axios.com/2022/09/21/rural-hospitals-face-funding-cliff/.

149 Lauren Weber, Laura Ungar, Michelle R. Smith, Hannah Recht, and Anna Maria Barry-Jester, "Hollowed-Out Public Health System Faces More Cuts Amid Virus, *Kaiser Health News*, July 1, 2020, https://khn.org/news/us-public-health-system-underfunded-under-threat-faces-more-cuts-amid-covid-pandemic/.

150 "National Diabetes Statistics Report 2020: Estimates of Diabetes and Its Burden in the United States," Centers for Disease Control and Prevention, 2020, https://www.cdc.gov/diabetes/pdfs/data/statistics/national-diabetes-statistics-report.pdf/.

151 "Disability and Diabetes Prevention," Centers for Disease Control and Prevention, accessed December 6, 2022, https://www.cdc.gov/ncbddd/disabilityandhealth/features/disability-and-diabetes-prevention.html/.

152 "Diabetes Self-Management for People with Disabilities and Type 2 Diabetes," Oregon Office on Disability and Health, accessed December 6, 2022, https://www.ohsu.edu/oregon-office-on-disability-and-health/diabetes-self-management-people-disabilities-and-type-2/.

153 Linda S. Geiss, Yanfeng Li, Israel Hora, Ann Albright, Deborah Rolka, and Edward W. Gregg, "Resurgence of Diabetes-Related Nontraumatic Lower-Extremity Amputation in the Young and Middle-Aged Adult U.S. Population," *Diabetes*, 42, no 1 (January 2019), https://diabetesjournals.org/care/article/42/1/50/36321/Resurgence-of-Diabetes-Related-Nontraumatic-Lower/.

154 Philip P. Goodney, MD, MS; Nino Dzebisashvili, PhD; David C. Goodman, MD, MS; and Kristen K. Bronner, MA; "Variation in the Care of Surgical Conditions: Diabetes and Peripheral Arterial Disease," The Dartmouth Atlas Project, 2014, https://www.diabetesincontrol.com/wp-content/uploads/2014/10/www.dartmouthatlas.org_downloads_reports_Diabetes_report_10_14_14.pdf/.

155 Lizzie Presser, "The Black American Amputation Epidemic," *ProPublica*, May 19, 2020, https://features.propublica.org/diabetes-amputations/black-american-amputation-epidemic/.

156 Eliana Block and Evan Koslof, "Yes, Insulin Costs About $10 to Make but Sells for Nearly $300," *WUSA9*, April 29, 2022, https://www.wusa9.com/article/news/verify/insulin-costs-about-10-to-make-but-retails-for-nearly-300-pharmaceutical-companies-eli-lilly-novo-nordisk-sanofi-pbms-insuli/65-73a3cafd-3340-45cd-8324-a5e3e1c78fa5/.

157 Angela Har, Samantha Young, "California Rx: State May Dive into Generic Drug Market," *KFF News*, September 1, 2020, California Rx: State May Dive Into Generic Drug Market - KFF Health News/.

158 Kenny Stancil, "Amid Eli Lilly-Twitter Fiasco, Groups Call for End to Insulin Price Gouging," *Common Dreams*, November 14, 2022, https://www.commondreams.org/news/2022/11/14/amid-eli-lilly-twitter-fiasco-groups-call-end-insulin-price-gouging/.

159 Mallory Locklear, "Insulin is an Extreme Financial Burden for Over 14% of Americans Who use it," Yale News, July 5, 2022, https://news.yale.edu/2022/07/05/insulin-extreme-financial-burden-over-14-americans-who-use-it/.

160 Jake Johnson, "'A Policy Failure': 1.3 Million US Adults With Diabetes Ration Insulin Due to High Cost," *Common Dreams*, October 18, 2022, https://www.commondreams.org/news/2022/10/18/policy-failure-13-million-us-adults-diabetes-ration-insulin-due-high-cost/.

161 Elizabeth Pfiester, Katarina Braune, Axel Thieffry, Hanne Ballhausen, Katarzyna Anna Gajewska, and Shane O'Donnell, "Costs and Underuse of Insulin and Diabetes Supplies: Findings from the 2020 T1 International Cross-sectional Web-based Survey," *Diabetes Research and Clinical Practice* 179, September 2021, https://www.sciencedirect.com/science/article/pii/S0168822721003557/.

162 Joseph Biden, "Executive Order on Lowering Prescription Drug Costs for Americans," The White House, October 14, 2022, https://www.whitehouse.gov/briefing-room/presidential-actions/2022/10/14/executive-order-on-lowering-prescription-drug-costs-for-americans/.

163 Gina Kolata, "These Doctors Admit They Don't Want Patients with Disabilities," *New York Times*, October 19, 2022, https://www.nytimes.com/2022/10/19/health/doctors-patients-disabilities.html/.

Chapter Six: A Glimpse into a Liberating Future

164 Nikolai Semashko, "The Work of the People's Commissariat of Health," *Soviet Russia* 3, no. 2 (September 18, 1920): 278; Arthur Newsholme and John Adams Kingsbury, *Red Medicine: Socialized Health in Soviet Russia* (New York: Doubleday, 1933), 276–277.

165 B. Gindis, Ph.D, "Vygotsky's Vision: Reshaping the Practice of Special Education for the 21st Century," *Remedial and Special Education* 20, no. 6, (1999): 32–64, http://www.bgcenter.com/Vygotsky_Vision.htm/; Estevan Hernandez, "A field Manual for Organizers: A Review of Revolutionary Education," *Liberation News*, January 18, 2022, https://www.liberationnews.org/a-field-manual-for-organizers-a-review-of-revolutionary-education/.

166 "499. Memorandum From the Deputy Assistant Secretary of State for Inter-American Affairs (Mallory) to the Assistant Secretary of State for Inter-American Affairs (Rubottom)," April 6, 1960, Department of State, Central Files, 737.00/4–660. Secret. Drafted by Lester Mallory, https://history.state.gov/historicaldocuments/frus1958-60v06/d499/.

167 Manolo De Los Santos and Vijay Prashad, "Guest Analysis: The United States Tries to Take Advantage of the Price Cubans are Paying for the Blockade and the Pandemic," *Liberation News*, July 13, 2021, https://www.liberationnews.org/the-united-states-tries-to-take-advantage-of-the-price-cubans-are-paying-for-the-blockade-and-the-pandemic/.

168 Rachell Tucker, "Supermajority of Cubans Vote for Revolutionary 'Families Code,'" *Liberation News*, September 27, 2022, https://www.liberationnews.org/supermajority-of-cubans-vote-for-revolutionary-families-code/.

169 Ibid.

170 Yaditza del Sol González, "How Does the New Family Code Protect Persons with Disabilities?," *Granma*, September 5, 2022, https://en.granma.cu/cuba/2022-09-05/how-does-the-new-family-code-protect-persons-with-disabilities.

171 "Cuban Families Code 2022 – Summary," trans. Walter Lippman, (Havana: Cultura Popular, 2022), https://walterlippmann.com/cuban-families-code-2022-summary/.

172 "The Committee on the Rights of Persons with Disabilities Reviews the Report of Cuba," United Nations Human Rights Office of the High Commissioner, March 27, 2019, https://www.ohchr.org/en/press-releases/2019/03/committee-rights-persons-disabilities-reviews-report-cuba/.

173 "Cuba's Family Code Enhances Recognition of Rights of Persons with Disabilities," CubaSí, January 27, 2022, https://cubasi.cu/en/news/cubas-family-code-enhances-recognition-rights-persons-disabilities/.

174 González, "How does the new Family Code Protect Persons with Disabilities?"

175 "The Committee on the Rights of Persons with Disabilities reviews the report of Cuba," United Nations Human Rights Office of the High Commissioner, March 27, 2019, https://www.ohchr.org/en/press-releases/2019/03/committee-rights-persons-disabilities-reviews-report-cuba/.

176 González, "How does the new Family Code Protect Persons with Disabilities?"

177 Lippman, "Cuban Families Code 2022 – Summary."

178 "Piden ley que proteja a las personas con discapacidad en Cuba," AdnCuba, December 19, 2019, https://adncuba.com/noticias-de-cuba/piden-ley-que-proteja-las-personas-con-discapacidad-en-cuba/.

179 Tomás Cardoso, "Discapacitados enfrentan carencias de todo tipo en Cuba," *Radio Television Marti*, September 17, 2018, https://www.radiotelevisionmarti.com/a/discapacitados-enfrentan-carencias-de-todo-tipo-en-cuba/210461.html/.

180 German Lopez, "Homeless in America," *New York Times*, July 15, 2022, https://www.nytimes.com/2022/07/15/briefing/homelessness-america-housing-crisis.html/.

181 Michael Maharrey, "Millions of Americans Face Eviction in Coming Months," SchiffGOLD, August 31, 2022, https://schiffgold.com/key-gold-news/millions-of-americans-face-eviction-in-coming-months/.

182 Jill Hamberg, "Cuba Opens to Private Housing but Preserves Housing Rights," Reimagine, Fall 2011, https://www.reimaginerpe.org/19-1/hamberg/.

183 "The Cuban Healthcare System," CubaPlatform, accessed December 7, 2022, https://cubaplatform.org/health carehealthcare/.

184 "Physicians per 1,000 People," World Bank, accessed March 18, 2024, https://data.worldbank.org/indicator/SH.MED.PHYS.ZS/.

185 "Cuba Has 9 Doctors Per 1000 Citizens, Highest in Its History," *teleSURHD*, July 23, 2019, https://www.telesurenglish.net/news/cuba-cuban-doctors-highest-number-in-history-20190723-0009.html.

186 C. William Keck, MD, MPH, "Health Equity, Cuban Style," *American Medical Association Journal of Ethics* 23, no. 3 (2021): E258–264, https://journalofethics.ama-assn.org/article/health-equity-cuban-style/2021-03/.

187 "The Cuban Healthcare System," CubaPlatform, accessed December 7, 2022, https://cubaplatform.org/health carehealthcare/.

188 Patricia Grogg, "Cuba's Inclusion Effort for Disabled," *Havana Times*, August 6, 2009, https://havanatimes.org/features/cubas-inclusion-effort-for-disabled/.

189 Alejandro Brice, "Comparative Policy Brief: Status of Intellectual Disabilities in the Republic of Cuba," *Journal of Policy and Practice in Intellectual Disabilities* 5, no.2 (June 2008): 118–121, doi:10.1111/j.1741-1130.2008.00157.x./.

190 "Cuba, Reference in Preventing and Treating Diabetes," *CubaPlus*, accessed December 7, 2022, https://www.cubaplusmagazine.com/en/news/cuba-reference-preventing-treating-diabetes.html/; Jorge Ruiz Miyares, "Cuba Stands Out as the First Country in Latin America in Diabetes Control," *Radio Havana Cuba*, January 14, 2020, https://www.radiohc.cu/en/noticias/salud/211870-cuba-stands-out-as-the-first-country-in-latin-america-in-diabetes-control/.

191 Ivan Martínez, "Cuba Reduces Risk of Amputation for Diabetes," *Radio Havana Cuba*, September 24, 2014, https://www.radiohc.cu/en/noticias/nacionales/34527-cuba-reduces-risk-of-amputation-for-diabetes/.

192 Juan Leandro, "Over 80 Percent of Cuban Diabetes Patients Prevented from Lower Limb Amputation," *Radio Havana Cuba*, November, 13, 2013, https://www.radiohc.cu/en/noticias/nacionales/5555-over-80-percent-of-cuban-diabetes-patients-prevented-from-lower-limb-amputation/.

193 Mario Hernandez, "Democratic Power of the People at the Heart of Cuban Socialism," *Liberation News*, September 13, 2022, https://www.liberationnews.org/democratic-power-of-the-people-at-the-heart-of-cuban-socialism/.

**Chapter Seven: A Socialist United States and the
Liberation of People with Disabilities**

194 Anshu Siripurapu, "The U.S. Inequality Debate," Council on Foreign Relations, April 20, 2022, https://www.cfr.org/backgrounder/us-inequality-debate/.

195 "Health Insurance Companies Make Record Profits as Costs Soar in US," WCSC TV, February 3, 2022, https://www.live5news.com/2022/02/03/health-insurance-companies-make-record-profits-costs-soar-us/.

196 "Medical Bills: The Leading Cause of Bankruptcy in the United States," Therapy Brand, May 25, 2018, Medical Bills: The Leading Cause of Bankruptcy in the United States | Therapy Brands.

197 Howard E. LeWine, "Millions of Adults Skip Medications Due to Their High Cost," *Harvard Health Publishing*, January 30, 2015, https://www.health.harvard.edu/blog/millions-skip-medications-due-to-their-high-cost-201501307673/.

198 Michael Sainato, "The Americans Dying because They Can't Afford Medical Care," *The Guardian*, January 7, 2020, https://www.theguardian.com/us-news/2020/jan/07/americans-healthcare-medical-costs/.

199 Mona Chalabi, "Will Losing Health Insurance Mean More US Deaths? Experts Say Yes," *The Guardian*, June 24, 2017, https://www.theguardian.com/us-news/2017/jun/24/us-healthcare-republican-bill-no-coverage-death/.

200 "Cost of Home: 2022 State of the Nation's Housing report," Habitat for Humanity, accessed March 1, 2023, https://www.habitat.org/costofhome/2022-state-nations-housing-report-lack-affordable-housing/.

201 Jaboa Lake, Valerie Novack, and Mia Ives-Rublee, "Recognizing and Addressing Housing Insecurity for Disabled Renters," Center for American Progress, May 21, 2021, https://www.americanprogress.org/article/recognizing-addressing-housing-insecurity-disabled-renters/.

202 Anissa Durham, "Most Americans are One Crisis Away from Becoming Unhoused," *San Diego Voice & Viewpoint*, January 5, 2023, https://sdvoice.info/most-americans-are-one-crisis-away-from-becoming-unhoused/.

203 German Lopez, "Homeless in America," *New York Times*, July 15, 2022, https://www.nytimes.com/2022/07/15/briefing/homelessness-america-housing-crisis.html/.

204 Craig Anthony, "10 Countries With the Most Natural Resources," *Investopedia*, September 23, 2023,https://www.investopedia.com/articles/markets-economy/090516/10-countries-most-natural-resources.asp/.

205 Sean Ross, "Four Countries that Produce the Most Food," *Investopedia*, December 17, 2023, https://www.investopedia.com/articles/investing/100615/4-countries-produce-most-food.asp/.

206 Testimony before the House Committee on Science, Space and Technology by Dr. Mehmood Khan on 6 March 2019, https://insight.ieeeusa.org/articles/maintaining-u-s-leadership-in-science-and-technology/.

207 "What Country Leads the World in Medical Innovation," Vantage Medtech, accessed March 18, 2024, https://vantagemedtech.com/what-country-leads-the-world-in-medical-innovation/?utm_source=sterlingmedicaldevices.com&utm_medium=referral/.

208 "Top Three Pressing Issues for Americans with Disabilities," *The Chicago Lighthouse*, accessed March 1, 2023, https://chicagolighthouse.org/sandys-view/top-three-pressing-issues-for-americans-with-disabilities/.

209 Russell Poole, "Billionaire's Row: The Empty Houses We Can Never Afford," CitySignal, November 15, 2022, https://www.citysignal.com/billionaires-row-the-empty-houses-we-can-never-afford/.

210 "Assessing the Accessibility of America's Housing Stock for Physically Disabled Persons," Office Of Policy Development and Research, Housing and Urban Development, accessed March 1, 2023, https://www.huduser.gov/portal/pdredge/pdr_edge_research_101315.html/.

211 Lake, Novack and Ives-Rublee, "Recognizing and Addressing Housing Insecurity for Disabled Renters."